SOUTH WEST COAST PATH

Falmouth to Exmouth

SOUTH WEST COAST PATH

Falmouth to Exmouth

Brian Le Messurier

Photographs by Mike Williams

AURUM PRESS

The Countryside Agency

ACKNOWLEDGEMENTS

The opportunity to write this guide seemed particularly apposite. Both my mother and grandfather were born at St Anthony Lighthouse at the west end of this stretch of the Coast Path. I work for the National Trust producing publications about its coastal properties in Devon and Cornwall, and live in Exeter, which sits astride the Exe, the eastern terminus of that section of the Coast Path covered by this book.

Ten years ago I wrote the first-generation official guide book to the *South Devon Coast Path*, but that book, and the series of which it was a part, is vastly out of date, so a new, consumer-orientated set of guide books was necessary for the many more people who now walk the Coast Path.

I am grateful to the following for assistance: the staff of the National Trust in Devon and Cornwall, the officers of the South Devon and South Cornwall Heritage Coast Services, the several kind friends who ferried me back to the start of my walking stints, and the others who provided companionship along the way and that vital second car on the longer sections.

B. Le M., 1990

The publisher would like to thank Mark Camp for his help in checking the route description for the 2003 edition.

This revised edition first published 2003 by Aurum Press Ltd in association with the Countryside Agency
Text copyright © 1990, 1996, 1999, 2001, 2003 by Aurum Press Ltd, the Countryside Agency and the Ordnance Survey
Photographs copyright © 1990, 1996 by the Countryside Agency / Mike Williams

A catalogue record for this book is available from the British Library.

ISBN 1 85410 890 5

Book design by Robert Updegraff

Cover photograph: The South West Coast Path near Polperro
Title page photograph: Looking north from Babbacombe
Both photographs copyright © 2002 by the Countryside Agency / Andrew Besley

Printed and bound in Italy by Printer Trento Srl

CONTENTS

Circular walks appear on pages 32, 48, 92, 104 and 126

HOW TO USE THIS GUIDE

The 630-mile (1014-kilometre) South West Coast Path is covered by four National Trail Guides. This book describes the Coast Path from Falmouth to Exmouth, 172 miles (277 kilometres). Companion guides describe the Coast Path from Minehead to Padstow, from Padstow to Falmouth, and from Exmouth to Poole. Each guide therefore covers a section of the Coast Path between major estuaries, where walkers may need a ferry or other transport.

This guide is in three parts:
• The introduction, including historical background to the area and advice for walkers.
• The Coast Path itself, described in eleven chapters, with maps opposite each route description. This part of the guide also includes information on places of interest as well as six circular walks spaced out along the Path, three in the Cornish section, and three in Devon, starting either from the Coast Path or at an inland car park. Key sites are numbered in the text and on the maps to make it easy to follow the route description.
• The last part includes useful information, such as local transport, ferries and river crossings, accommodation, organisations involved with the Coast Path, and further reading.

The maps have been prepared by the Ordnance Survey using 1:25 000 Explorer® or Outdoor Leisure® maps as a base. The line of the Coast Path is shown in yellow, with the status of each section of the Coast Path – footpath or bridleway for example – shown in green underneath (see key on inside front cover). These rights of way markings also indicate the precise alignment of the Coast Path, which walkers should follow. In some cases the yellow line on these maps may show a route which is different from that shown on older maps. Walkers are then recommended to follow the yellow route in this guide, which is that waymarked with the distinctive acorn symbol 🌰 used for all National Trails. Any parts of the Coast Path that may be difficult to follow on the ground are clearly highlighted in the route description, and important points to watch for are marked with letters in each chapter, both in the text and on the maps. *Black arrows* (➔) *at the edge of the maps indicate the start point.* Should there have been a need to alter the route since the publication of this guide, walkers are advised to follow the signs which have been erected on site to indicate this.

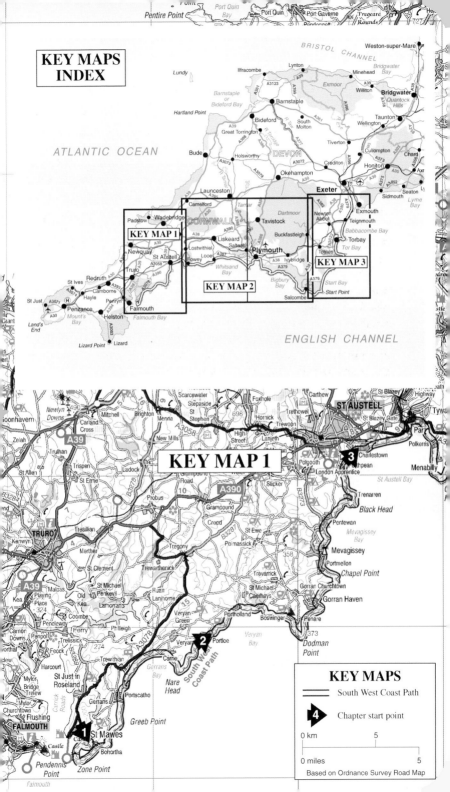

Distance checklist

This list will assist you in calculating the distances between places on the Coast Path where you may be planning to stay overnight, or in checking your progress along the way.

location	*approx. distance from previous location*	
	miles	km
Place (south side of Percuil River)	0	0
Portscatho	6.4	10.3
Portloe	7.2	11.6
Gorran Haven	8.4	13.5
Mevagissey	3.3	5.3
Charlestown	6.9	11.1
Polkerris	5.5	8.9
Fowey (Fowey Harbour – west)	4.6	7.4
Polruan (Fowey Harbour – east)	0	0
Polperro	6.9	11.1
Looe (bridge joining East and West Looe)	5.0	8.1
Portwrinkle	7.7	12.4
Kingsand / Cawsand	10.0	16.1
Cremyll (west side of ferry across Tamar)	3.3	5.3
Stonehouse (Plymouth)	0	0
Turnchapel (Plymouth)	6.9	11.1
Warren Point (Wembury) (Yealm Estuary – west)	7.8	12.6
Noss Mayo (Yealm Estuary – east)	0	0
Wonwell (Erme Estuary – east)	9.2	14.8
Cockleridge (Avon Estuary – west)	6.1	9.8
Bantham (Avon Estuary – east)	0	0
Salcombe (Salcombe Harbour – west)	12.3	19.8
East Portlemouth (Salcombe Harbour – east)	0	0
Torcross	13.5	21.7
Dartmouth (Dartmouth Harbour – west)	10.2	16.4
Kingswear (Dartmouth Harbour – east)	0	0
Brixham	11.2	18.0
Torquay Harbour	8.4	13.5
Shaldon (Teign Estuary – south)	11.3	18.2
Teignmouth (Teign Estuary – north)	0	0
Starcross (Exe Estuary – west)	7.6	12.2

PREFACE

The South West Coast Path National Trail is a 630-mile adventure around the coastline of the south-west peninsula. From Minehead on the edge of the Exmoor National Park all the way to the shores of Poole Harbour, it is simply the best way to enjoy this wonderful coastline, its scenery, wildlife and history.

Between Falmouth and Exmouth the Trail takes in some of Britain's most popular beaches and resorts as well as one or two major towns. Despite this the Coast Path walker will also be able to explore some of the least well-known stretches of the coast of Devon and Cornwall. Between the busy towns and villages are dramatic cliffs and headlands (for example, the Dodman, Rame Head or Start Point), sandy beaches and sheltered coves – some accessible only to people on foot. And then there are the spectacular 'drowned' estuaries such as the Fal, Yealm or Dart, so characteristic of this coastline and each with its own atmosphere. The walker crosses these by ferry, stepping stones or simply wading.

The Countryside Agency is proud of its role in creating and being the major funder of the South West Coast Path. Enjoyed by millions of people every year – both local residents and visitors – it offers relaxation and challenge, tranquillity and inspiration. Whether you are about to stroll out on the cliffs from Polperro or Dartmouth, or walk all the way from Falmouth to Exmouth, I hope you too will discover – or rediscover – the endless fascination of the South West Coast Path.

Ewen Cameron
Chairman
Countryside Agency

PART ONE

INTRODUCTION

INTRODUCTION

by John Macadam

On the edge of the land

The South West Coast Path must be one of the most spectacular and varied long-distance trails in the world. And at 630 miles (just over 1000 kilometres), from Minehead to Poole, it is certainly Britain's longest. Never far from the sea, the route will take the walker high above the shore and then swoop down to a fishing village in a cove. In fact, someone has calculated that if you walk those 630 miles, you will also climb three times the height of Everest! Not that you will need extra oxygen, of course, though wind-proof insulated clothing can be much appreciated if you are walking into a sou'westerly gale. At other times a T-shirt is more appropriate. But more about that later.

The Trail will take you through historic towns and villages, through woods, fields and sand dunes, and alongside quiet creeks and past streams falling from high cliffs into the sea. Occasionally you will walk through a busy town, but often there will be more wildlife – the inevitable gulls, but maybe also seals, basking sharks, dolphins, or choughs – than humans. To refresh yourself there are local beers, clotted-cream teas, Cornish pasties, Ruby Red steaks and Dorset Blue cheese, and smoked mackerel. Or you could sample the industrial heritage: pilchard 'palaces' and mining in Cornwall, or quarrying on Portland. If none of that takes your fancy, there are more ethereal pleasures: literary associations, from Daniel Defoe to John Fowles, connections with artists from Turner to Kurt Jackson, the Cornish language ('Kernewek') and innumerable Celtic saints. And if you do not like beer, there's a range of ciders made from traditional varieties of apples in Somerset and Devon, and even a few recently planted vineyards near the Path.

For centuries, local people would have used paths along the coast for many purposes, including gathering food and looking for wreckage. But in the eighteenth century the government imposed high import duties on a range of luxury goods, precipitating a rapid growth in smuggling – and yet another use for the paths. The official response was draconian legislation prohibiting anyone from 'lurking, waiting or loitering within five miles from the sea-coast', but the trade was too lucrative to suppress. Finally, in the early nineteenth century, the coastguard service was set up, with men patrolling nightly, and so a continuous coast path developed. The coastguards had to be able to look down into coves and narrow inlets, so their route was truly at the edge of the cliffs. But by the early 1800s, a few visitors were using the path for leisure, even if they sometimes had to prove that they had no other purpose!

Use of much of this path was lost, not, as might be expected, by natural geological processes, but by landowners, often backed by the courts, prohibiting access. In 1949 the Act which set up National Parks in England and Wales also set up long-distance paths, including one around the South West Peninsula. The Path was opened in stages, with the last major section opened in 1978, and the patient operation to reinstate the route along the coast is now nearly complete.

Geological processes have indeed destroyed the old coastguards' tracks in many places, and those same processes are no respecters of hard-won modern routes, so realignment is an ongoing task. Active erosion also means that the geology is exposed in many places, not clothed in soil and vegetation as inland, so the walker will see an impressive range of strata, folds, faults, intrusions, stacks, and caves – a real tour de force. Indeed, a 95-mile stretch of the coast, in East Devon and Dorset, is designated a World Heritage Site for the global scientific importance of its exposure of 185 million years of the Mesozoic Era. This is the icing on the cake, for much of the Path passes through areas with one or more national designations for landscape, wildlife, or geology: National Park, National Nature Reserve, Heritage Coast, Area of Outstanding Natural Beauty, Site of Special Scientific Interest, and others. But you do not have to be an expert (or understand all these designations!) to enjoy all the flowers, butterflies and birds you will see at different times of the year.

Management of the Path requires great sensitivity to potentially competing interests. Funded primarily by the Countryside Agency, this task is shared between approximately 70 staff working for six highway authorities (or their agents), the Ministry of Defence, and the National Trust, and co-ordinated by the South West Coast Path Team based in Exeter. Day-to-day work includes cutting back vegetation, clearing drainage ditches, and replacing broken stiles and signs. In addition to routine maintenance, South West Coast Path managers strive to provide the best experience by realigning sections that involve road walking or re-routing the Path as quickly as possible after cliff falls have taken place.

Planning your walk

You may be planning to walk the whole length of the Path, or you may just intend to walk a short distance. Even a walk along the promenade is likely to be a walk along the Coast Path! Some of the Path can be enjoyed by people who are less mobile, but very little can be used by cyclists or horse-riders.

If you are planning short walks, there are many circular routes to get you back to your starting point, and in many places there is public transport (but make sure you take the bus or train to your furthest point, then walk back, or else leave yourself plenty of time).

Whatever walk you plan, be sure you are fit enough, particularly if you are planning to walk for several days consecutively. Remember those three Everests! Some people walk the whole Path in one go, and most take 50–60 days to do this. A few people have taken far less time, but they must have missed out a great deal.

The best time to walk the Path is probably May–June, with long days, masses of wild flowers and few people. Another good time is September, when most of the summer visitors have gone. Since the area relies heavily on tourism, there is a wide range of accommodation, from camp sites, youth hostels, B&Bs (bed & breakfast) to rather grand hotels, though everywhere can become full at the height of the tourist season in July and August and it is wise to book ahead. If you intend to camp away from a recognised campsite, you will need to ask permission of the landowner, usually the local farmer, and remember to leave no trace of your stay.

If you plan to walk between October and April, you may have the luxury of the Coast Path to yourself. You may also find some ferries are not running and public services, like buses and trains, are running a restricted winter schedule. Tourist Information Centres (TICs), the information section at the back of this book and the National Trail website (www.national-trail.co.uk) will either provide the necessary information or give you the necessary contacts.

Equipment

British weather is notorious for its changeability, and the weather in the South West is generally wetter, windier and warmer than most of Britain. Most of the Coast Path is very exposed to the elements; the exceptions are some of the estuaries. The relative exposure depends on which way the wind is coming from – the prevailing wind is southwesterly – and which way the coast faces. The effects of wind chill can be extreme: wind chill is caused by the wind evaporating moisture from your skin.

With all this in mind, it makes sense to get a weather forecast (from the media, by telephone or the web) and be prepared. It is always sensible to carry a wind-proof waterproof: the breathable ones are best, and the reproofable ones with a lifetime guarantee are the best of all.

There are various types of walking trousers, though most people use quick-drying polycotton fabrics, with waterproof overtrousers. Denim is decidedly unwise as when wet it becomes stiff and heavy, and is also very slow to dry, thus increasing the risk of hypothermia. A hat of some form is recommended, and a supply of sunscreen to be applied in good time to your neck, arms and anywhere else that is exposed. Traditionally, strong shoes or walking boots with good grips have always been recommended, though some people are very happy wearing sandals designed for walkers.

Finally, walkers need to take an adequate supply of liquid, a whistle and a first-aid kit, all in a rucksack which is adjusted to fit the wearer comfortably. Of course, long-distance walkers will have far more to carry than this, but will take trouble to minimise the weight. Some companies and B&B owners will transport your pack for you to your next stop, for a fee, so that all you need to carry is a daypack. Cash machines are only to be found in the larger towns, so paying bills and withdrawing cash can be a problem, especially for visitors without a sterling cheque account.

Finding your way

The sign for all National Trails is a stylised acorn, and you will find this cut into wooden waymarks, chiselled into stone waymarks, cast in metal, and stuck to aluminium road signs. Most signs also bear the words 'Coast Path'.

You should have few problems following the acorns and thus the Trail. The route is also shown on the maps in this guidebook. You may find that the route has changed from that shown on the maps, in which case follow the acorns and any diversion signs. The reason for the latter may well be a cliff-fall, or the Path starting to crumble away. It is obviously foolhardy to ignore diversion signs.

Safety

The main safety message is: keep to the Path. The Path is close to the edge of the cliff in many places. Make sure you are suitably equipped both for your walk and for changing weather conditions.

Those who go down to beaches and rocks beside the sea need to be aware of the tides, with around 9 metres between high and low tide at Minehead, though only a couple of metres at Poole. Every year people get cut off by the tide and have to be rescued. People also get washed off rocks by so-called 'freak waves'. At many places around this coastline you can watch surfers waiting for the bigger waves.

Bathing too can be hazardous, chiefly because of currents. It is best only to swim in safe areas patrolled by lifeguards, who are only employed in the summer. Many beaches have rip currents which drain most of the water that comes onto the beach. If you get caught in a rip current, do not try to swim against it, but rather swim diagonally across it until you are in stiller water, when it is safe to swim back to the beach.

If you do get into difficulties on the Path, the international alarm call is six long blasts on a whistle, followed by one minute's silence.

The coastguards are responsible for dealing with any emergency that occurs on the coast or at sea. Please remember that there are no coastguard lookouts now, and the service relies on the watchful eyes of the public. If you see vessels or people you think are in distress, dial 999 (or 112 on a mobile) and ask for the coastguard. Beneath some cliffs there may be no mobile signal.

The Act forbidding 'lurking, waiting or loitering within five miles from the sea-coast' was repealed in 1825, so relax, explore and enjoy the South West Coast Path and the coasts of Somerset, Devon, Cornwall and Dorset.

PART TWO

SOUTH WEST COAST PATH

Falmouth to Exmouth

1 Crossing the Fal, and on to Portloe

from Place via Portscatho
13½ miles (21.7 km)

The challenges on the Coast Path between the Fal and the Exe begin as soon as you reach St Mawes **1** via the year-round ferry from Falmouth. The ferry service from St Mawes to Place, the true commencement of this stretch of path, only operates from May to September. However, there is a water taxi that may be able to take you across out of season (see ferry and river crossings section, pages 157–60). If the water taxi is not running, it is a walk of at least 8 miles (13 km) around the head of the Percuil River, involving a certain amount of road walking. The only other option is to catch the bus from St Mawes to Porthscatho and then walk to Place, partly using the circular route described on page 32.

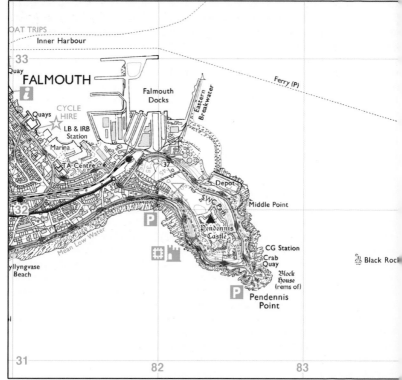

Contours are given in me
The vertical interval is 5

While contemplating this next step it is worth taking a look at St Mawes, which is much more than a stepping stone on the Coast Path. Once a fishing village (with a pilotage speciality), like several dozen others on the Cornish coast, St Mawes has gone upmarket in the last 80 years, and is now one of the county's premier yachting centres.

A 10-minute walk to the west of the harbour is St Mawes Castle, a well-preserved fortification built by Henry VIII in 1538 when he began to look to the nation's coastal defences after his excommunication. The plan imitates a clover leaf, and the keep is mounted atop the trefoil. Across the water is Pendennis Castle, Henry's other castle in this area. St Mawes Castle is owned by English Heritage and is open at the times advertised.

If you are walking east-to-west to Place and want to cross to St Mawes out of season, you must not expect to find an obliging boatman prepared to act as ferryman, and there is not even a phone box from which to call a taxi. You should make plans

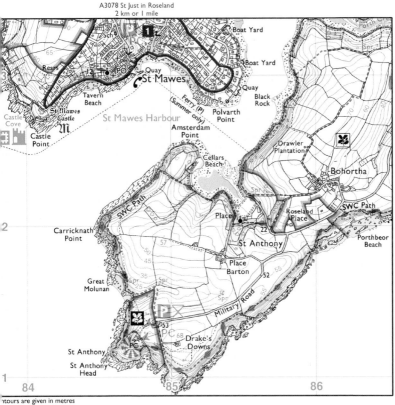

ntours are given in metres
he vertical interval is 5m

for your onward progress before reaching the end of the Coast Path, and Portscatho or its neighbour Gerrans are the places to do this. A glance at the map may tempt the east-to-west walker to omit this remote headland south of Portscatho, but its very inaccessibility is one of its charms.

I will assume you have reached Place by whatever means. Totty's Steps is the landing for the ferry from St Mawes **1** and these are reached along the path on the east side of Place Creek, and a few yards inside Drawler Plantation.

There was at one time a public right of way across the creek from the slipway, but if the tide is in, the 'path' is under water, and if the tide is out, the path – which does not exist on the ground – would be a wet and muddy route, and anyone using it would miss seeing Place and St Anthony Church. So I advise you to take the official route up the lane past the gate to Place **2**, to a stile about 250 yards (230 metres) from the slipway on the west side of the lane. Climb the stile, and head for St Anthony Church **3**, noting how it is joined to Place House at the north transept. The south doorway is fine late-Norman work, and inside the tower the arches date from the 13th century. Nikolaus Pevsner thought it 'the best example in the county of what a parish church was like in the 12th or 13th centuries'.

Walk up the slope and steps opposite the fine Norman south door, join a farm track, and descend to the creek-side past Place House. The present French-looking building was constructed in 1840 on the site of an Elizabethan house, which itself replaced a priory. The lawn in front was created in the middle of the last century from the mill pond of a tide mill, and the present sea wall was built where the tide mill dam once stood.

Herons may be seen along here, standing motionless in the water, waiting for a small fish or crab to come along. Before reaching Cellars Cottages, climb a stile and ascend a field to another stile at the top. Cellars Cottages served as pilchard cellars where the fish were processed before being exported to the Catholic countries of southern Europe.

From the stile a panoramic view opens to the north-west. St Mawes with its castle occupies the middle distance, with Falmouth 2 miles (3.2 km) away across Carrick Roads. The hills on the skyline were part of Cornwall's rich mining country in the 1800s. A coast-to-coast trail runs from Devoran, a former port at the head of Restronguet Creek, to the harbour at Portreath on the north coast. Descend to the foot of the field, and follow the Coast Path around Carricknath Point.

The Coast Path crosses a wooden bridge over a concrete dam dating from 1914, built to form a reservoir to provide water for St Anthony Battery. The reservoir is now choked with silt. Below the dam are the small beaches of Great and Little Molunan, a lovely spot for a bathe at low tide.

Ignore the steep path climbing to the car park and stay low, entering a gate and contouring along a good path, past the old paraffin store, to St Anthony Lighthouse **4**. For safety's sake only enough fuel for its immediate needs was kept at the lighthouse, and the keepers carried it in churn-like containers suspended from wooden yokes. If time permits, and the lighthouse is open, a visit to climb the tower is strongly recommended.

The lighthouse was built in 1834, as much to warn seafarers of the deadly Manacles reef to the south as to indicate the entrance to Falmouth harbour. The squat structure lies close to the water's edge. From 1882 to 1954 a bell, the largest in Cornwall, hung from the exterior below the lantern, and was rung in foggy conditions.

From the lighthouse return for 50 yards (46 metres), climb the path to the car park and St Anthony Battery **5**, and turn right (south) at the top. On the outside wall of the toilets, note the interpretive panel describing the battery. The officers' quarters **6** have been converted by the National Trust into comfortable holiday

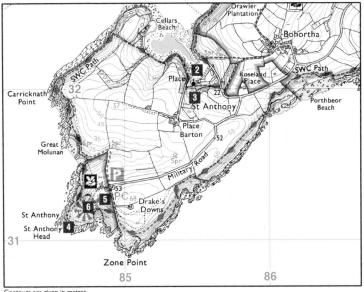

Contours are given in metres
The vertical interval is 5m

23

cottages, some of them suitable for disabled visitors. Old maps show a cliff castle or possibly a Roman signal station on the headland, but when the site was fortified in 1885 all traces of this earthwork disappeared.

On top of the gun apron the National Trust has erected a toposcope (viewfinder) which lines up places of interest and is accessible to people in wheelchairs. The Radford sisters, who are mentioned on the toposcope, were benefactors of the National Trust.

Leave this splendid viewpoint by heading south-east around Zone Point, the best place in the area for spotting sea birds. A prominent one-time coastguard signal station on Drake's Downs was demolished by the National Trust in 1985 as the wall ties had rusted through and rebuilding was uneconomical. The Coast Path follows the cliff edge with no fencing on the inland side, and this gives a feeling of freedom. It dips across a valley, and passes behind Porthbeor Beach, which is reached by a cliff path and linked to the nearby road by a short path.

Once past Porthbeor, the Coast Path wanders agreeably eastwards, turning north once round Killigerran Head, and reaches Towan Beach near a wreck post 7, a relic of the days when the breeches buoy was employed by the coastguard service in ship rescues. It is a sturdy pole with climbing steps which simulated the mast of a ship in training exercises. A rocket was fired at the pole, the rope made fast, and the breeches buoy brought into play.

Towan is Cornish for sand dune, but as none exist there today it is safe to assume that a combination of the removal of sand to spread on the land to lighten the soil, and the consequent erosion of the beach-back by the sea, has caused the loss of stability in the low cliffs behind the beach. A short path links the beach with a car park and toilets at Porth. This was once a sanding road 8. These are access tracks to beaches up which carts, packhorses and pannier-laden donkeys brought seaweed and sand to spread on the land as natural fertiliser. Over the years so much sand was removed that some Cornish beaches were seriously eroded.

North of Towan Beach the Coast Path keeps to the cliff edge and Portscatho 9 is reached without difficulty. Along this stretch you will see examples of the Cornish stile, a kind of stone cattle grid, and at the north end of Towan Beach there are three more sanding roads.

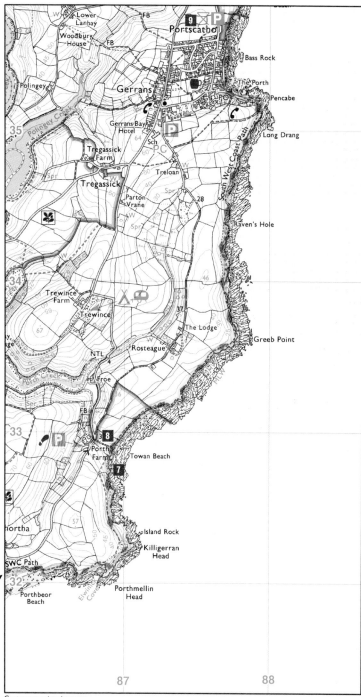

Lower Lanhay
Woodbury House
FB
9
Portscatho
P
Bass Rock
Polingey
Gerrans
The Porth
Pencabe
PO
Gerrans Bay Hotel
P
Long Drang
35
Polingey Creek
Sch
PC
64
Tregassick Farm
Treloan
60
South West Coast Path
Tregassick
Parton Vrane
28
Raven's Hole
Spr
Spr
34
46
Trewince Farm
59
37
67
Trewince
The Lodge
Greeb Point
NTL
Rosteague
Porth Creek
Froe
Spr
FB
33
P
8
Porth Farm
Towan Beach
7
hortha
57
Island Rock
Killigerran Head
SWC Path
32
Porthbeor Beach
Elwinick Cove
Porthmellin Head

87   88

Contours are given in metres
The vertical interval is 5m

25

Froe Creek tide mill pond, near Towan Beach.

Portscatho **9** is an east-facing fishing village that now enjoys a Siamese-twin existence with Gerrans, the ancient parish centre up the hill. It boasts a good pub and some interesting little shops.

Leave the village along North Parade and pass through several fields down-slope from the main Portscatho car park. The Coast Path goes down a flight of stone steps into a steep, gullied track that descends to Porthcurnick Beach, and at low tide you can stroll across the strand to pick up the Coast Path at the far side. The taking of sand so reduced the level of Porthcurnick Beach that some cottages and a lime kiln were destroyed by the sea. At high tide you must pass behind the beach.

At the top of Porthcurnick Beach slipway, take the Coast Path going round Pednvadan, proceed north through several fields before passing into a wood, then descending to Porthbean Beach. At exceptional high tides, in stormy conditions, the beach becomes washed by waves, so the walker must be aware of this risk.

Leaving the beach after only about 10 yards (9 metres), turn up and take a right, sea-side, fork quite soon, to pass an isolated chalet. The Coast Path then passes through several more fields before passing above some small coves, and past a gate bearing a sign saying 'Curgurrel Farm Harbour'. Do not be misled by the grand name; this is only a slip leading to a tiny cove.

The Coast Path soon enters the National Trust property known as Treluggan Cliff, a scrubby slope through which the route wanders beguilingly. At the far end it turns briefly inland to circumvent the Pendower Hotel. At the road, turn right (south-east) and follow it past a car park to the road-end at the Pendower Beach House Hotel.

Here a lime kiln and a Second World War pillbox stand forlornly beside a very popular and safe beach which is a designated Eurobeach, complying fully with European Union standards.

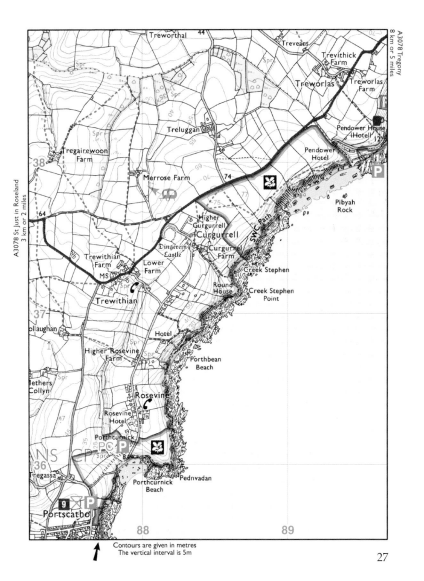

Contours are given in metres
The vertical interval is 5m

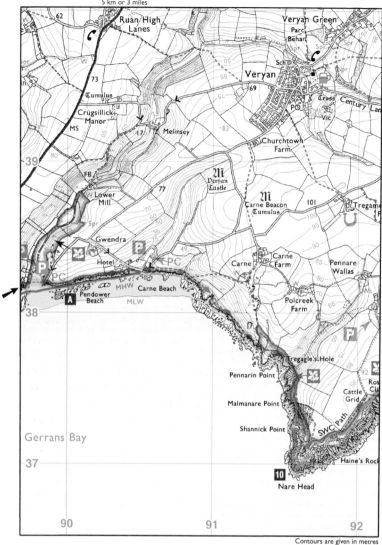

The route crosses the beach, or, at high tide, goes round the back of the beach to the car park, then climbs the road on the east side for a short distance before entering a field by a stile. This takes the walker along the low cliffs and in front of the Nare Hotel to the road near Carne Beach, where there is another large car park and two Second World War pillboxes, both rather hard to spot. At low tide, Pendower Beach and Carne Beach coalesce, forming one long stretch of sand nearly a mile (1.5 km) long, and it is hard to say where Pendower ends and Carne begins. Follow the beach **A** if you prefer.

From the back of the large car park serving Carne Beach, a National Trust permissive footpath goes up the field to the pre-historic site known as Veryan Castle. It is positioned on the side of a hill and was presumably a settlement of some kind, although no dwelling remains have been found. About 400 yards (365 metres) to the east is Carne Beacon, one of the largest Bronze Age barrows in Britain. An excavation in 1855 revealed a stone cairn on top of a large cist (burial chamber) which contained ashes and charcoal. This site can be visited from a public footpath that passes the barrow.

From Carne Beach go up the road to the east, and round the hairpin bend turn right (east) over a stile signposted 'Portloe'. The Coast Path goes through a succession of fields. At the end of the second, look up left at the rocky crag near Carne Farm. (*Carn* is Cornish for a tor, or natural pile of rocks.)

After a climb, the Coast Path descends steeply to Paradoe Cove (pronounced Prada) where a National Trust permissive path comes down the valley from the north-east. Paradoe Cove is marked on the OS map as Tregagle's Hole. On the south side of the cove stand the remains of a fisherman's cottage. Once of two storeys and probably thatched, the walls above the ground floor are of cob, a mixture of clay and straw. The Coast Path climbs steeply out of the valley, and soon the crags of Nare Head beckon **10**.

This is a fine headland bristling with exposed igneous rock at its tip. In 1540 it was called Penare Point, with the accent on the second syllable, but over the years the unstressed first syllable was dropped.

The National Trust, as owner, was responsible for a great deal of tidying up and rationalisation of the farming landscape on Nare Head a few years ago. The agricultural buildings were old, scattered and unsuitable for modern farming, so the Trust, with help from the Ministry of Agriculture, built a completely new complex of buildings for the tenant, nearer to his house and in a natural hollow. The redundant structures were cleared away, a car park was built for visitors, a view-point provided, suitable for disabled people, and a new path opened from the car park down to Paradoe Cove. Several hundred trees were planted in this valley. Gull Rock, three-quarters of a mile (1.2 km) east of Nare Head, is a noted seabird nesting site which was given to the National Trust in 1989.

The Coast Path skirts Nare Head, picks up a tractor track and goes north, then bears round the cliff edge and fence line.

Montbretia beside the Coast Path at Portloe.

Follow the waymarks down **B**, and around Kiberick Cove. The curiously contoured field here is believed to have slipped 'once upon a time' and is called Slip Field. The Coast Path now rounds the Blouth and drops almost to sea level at Parc Caragloose Cove where you cross over a stream before climbing up a bracken slope, with a few zigzags thrown in for good measure.

The Coast Path now stays high around Manare Point before dropping down past a spiney ridge called The Jacka to the cosy village of Portloe **11**, which you reach close to the toilets. This must rate as one of the most unspoilt and attractive fishing villages in the whole of Britain. Very little new building has taken place to spoil it. As a harbour it is very cramped, and this was one reason why in the 17 years that there was a lifeboat stationed at Portloe it did not perform a single service: in stormy weather the narrow entrance is too difficult for boats to negotiate.

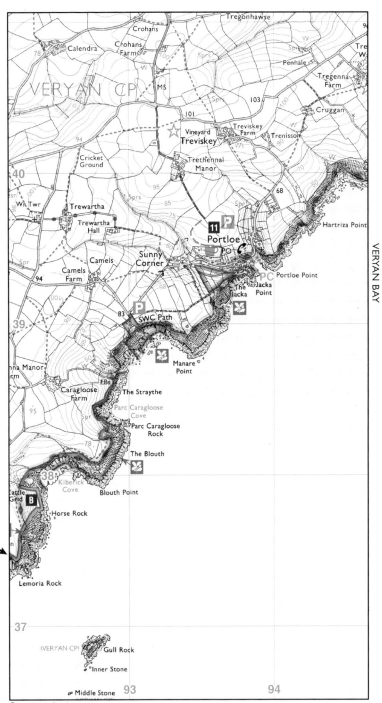

VERYAN BAY

A CIRCULAR WALK ROUND THE COAST AND CREEKS OF THE ROSELAND PENINSULA

5³/₄ miles (9.3 km)

From the National Trust car park at Porth, between Gerrans and St Anthony, walk down through the lower, grassy car parking area below and behind Towan Cottage. This leads to a footbridge over a stream, which gives access to a 2-mile (3.2-km) creekside path leading to Place slipway. At this point the beginning of the Coast Path is picked up (see page 22), and it may be followed past St Anthony Head and Zone Point, all the way round to Towan Beach, about another 4 miles (6.1 km). Turn inland here, and Porth car park is reached in 250 yards (230 metres).

Scale approx 1 inch to ½ mile

Contours are given in metres
The vertical interval is 5m

Conserving the Cornish and South Devon Coasts

The Coast Path is formally designated by the Countryside Agency with the blessing of the government, but it is managed by Cornwall and Devon County Councils with substantial help from the Agency.

Much of the countryside through which the Path runs has been formally designated as an Area of Outstanding Natural Beauty by the Agency. This gives national recognition to the high quality of the landscape.

Heritage Coasts

The need for measures to protect the undeveloped coast became a matter of some urgency just before the Second World War, when the ever-quickening pace of change was beginning to destroy the beauty of parts of Britain's rural coastline. During the war the government therefore appointed Professor Steers, the eminent coastal geographer, to assess the scenic quality of the unspoilt coastline of England and Wales.

It was more than 20 years before the government set in motion an official review. In 1970 the then Countryside Commission reported back with a major proposal that 'the most scenically outstanding stretches of undeveloped coast be defined and protected as Heritage Coasts'.

As much as 32 per cent (642 miles/1027 km) of scenic English coastline is now conserved as Heritage Coasts, thus affording special protection through planning and a strong emphasis on practical action.

Much of the coast of Cornwall and Devon has been so defined, and there are four stretches between Falmouth and Exmouth: the Roseland; Gribben Head to Polperro; Rame Head; and South Devon.

The National Trust

The National Trust (NT) is a charity, independent of government, founded in 1895 to acquire land and buildings for their permanent protection in England, Wales and Northern Ireland.

The Trust's first coastal acquisition in England was Barras Nose in North Cornwall in 1897, and the Dodman was given in 1919. Other properties followed in the 1920s and 1930s, but it was not until after the Second World War that, with the increasing threats to the coastline, the need quickened to acquire further stretches.

Looking east across the mouth of the Dart to the Mew Stone and Outer Froward

Thus the National Trust launched Enterprise Neptune (now called the Neptune Coastline Campaign) in 1965 to enable the acquisition of outstanding natural or historic coastal land. It has raised over £36 million and more than 413 miles (665 km) of coastline have been purchased.

As you walk the Coast Path the boundary signs announce the NT's interest in many of the most beautiful stretches of land, not necessarily just rough cliff land, but sometimes extending a mile or so inland and including whole farms.

These major acquisitions mean that the NT is able to manage the land to the great advantage of the public, the tenant farmers and the landscape. Discreet new car parks and permissive link

...int from Combe Point.

paths are provided, trees planted, and new farm buildings erected, tucked into the hillsides.

So that the public can get the maximum enjoyment out of NT land, a series of interpretive leaflets is published by the Devon and Cornwall Regional Offices. These provide maps of all the paths and considerable detail about the history and wildlife of the area. A number of interpretive panels are also provided at selected locations. The NT now owns 163 miles (261 km) of the Cornish coast, and 111 miles (178 km) of the Devon coast. A further 25 miles (40 km) and 10 miles (16 km) respectively is covenanted, meaning that 43 per cent of the Cornish coast and 59 per cent of the Devon coast is protected by the Trust.

2 Portloe to Charlestown

through Gorran Haven and Mevagissey
18½ miles (29.8 km)

Portloe **11** grew as a settlement where two valleys converge at a narrow break in the cliffs. In the northern valley is a converted Methodist chapel. The present building dates from 1882. A previous building was struck by lightning and badly damaged.

The Coast Path passes in front of the chapel **12** and some neighbouring cottages before climbing steeply to a small National Trust property known as the Old Flagstaff. Here an enclosure on the sea side of the Coast Path represents all that is left of an early-19th-century coastguard watch house.

The shattered craggy buttress of Hartriza Point is crossed. Like Nare Head and The Jacka it is composed of igneous rock, but this is the only obstacle to easy progress. A Shag Rock is passed offshore; there is another at St Anthony Head, but that

High tide at East Portholland. Note the double doors of the houses.

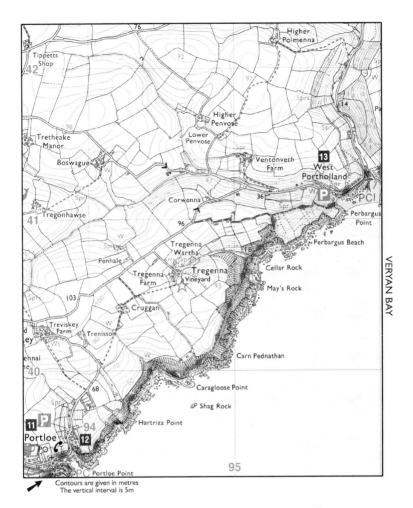

Contours are given in metres
The vertical interval is 5m

one is not shown on the map. You may like to note how repetitious some place names are as you progress eastwards. Usually several miles separate the same place name. Curiously, a Caragloose Point three-quarters of a mile (1.2 km) north-east of Portloe repeats a name found 1 mile (1.6 km) south-west of that village. As you near West Portholland you pass through an area that over the years has become covered in Japanese knotweed. This highly invasive plant takes up to ten years to eradicate; please keep to the path while the work is in progress.

The Coast Path descends to the twin villages of West and East Portholland **13**, each standing behind a beach and in its own valley. They are joined by a road along which the Coast Path is routed. West Portholland is the smaller of the two villages and

Caerhays Castle at Porthluney Cove.

consists of a Methodist chapel, a lime kiln, fishing sheds and a few dwellings. East Portholland is a little larger, and has a post office and shop, and used to have a pub called The Cutter. There was a Methodist chapel here, too, and mills once used the water flowing down the valleys. Note how the easternmost cottages in East Portholland are shuttered against breaking waves.

The Coast Path climbs up behind these cottages and follows a partly tarmaced path for some distance to a gate. Enter a field and turn right, descending down the field edge. As you walk along the bottom of the field, notice the building above you: this is an old coastguard watch house, which has been conserved in the last few years by the Countryside Stewardship scheme.

When you reach the end of the second field, the path follows the edge of the wood inland to the road. Turn right here and walk down to Porthluney Cove. After you meet the road and are walking down to the cove, the ruin visible from a gate and almost hidden in ivy and undergrowth is probably a folly. This is on private land and may be viewed only from the road.

Porthluney Cove is a clean and healthy stretch of sand, offering safe bathing, and is a designated Eurobeach. Behind the beach are the grounds of Caerhays Castle **14**. Designed in 1808 by John

Nash, who was responsible for Buckingham Palace and the Brighton Pavilion, this picturesque mansion stands in splendid grounds, which are sometimes open for charity.

Walk east behind the beach and turn right into parkland just after a lodge. The Coast Path climbs to the left of a wooded area, turning right behind the trees to reach a stile. Go around the next field to another stile, from where the path heads for Greeb Point.

National Trust land is entered at Lambsowden Cove, but Greeb Point is not Trust-owned. Once over the spine of Greeb

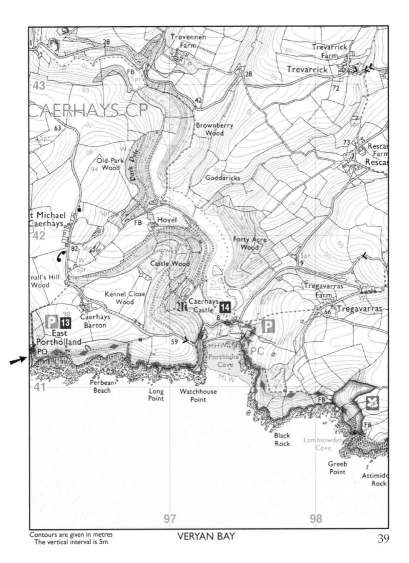

Contours are given in metres
The vertical interval is 5m
VERYAN BAY
39

Point the path is clear and pleasant as it rambles down (mostly) to Hemmick Beach. Boswinger Youth Hostel is half a mile (800 metres) up the road to the north.

Hemmick Beach is one of Cornwall's most beautiful coves. South-west-facing, with rock pools, sand and no commercialisation, it should be reached – if not by the Coast Path – by walking down from the National Trust car park in the hamlet of Penare. There is no room for cars behind the beach, and the approach lanes are narrow and exceedingly steep.

A few yards up the road to the south of Hemmick Beach, a stile gives access to the Coast Path once more. There is initially a steep climb, then the path levels out, dips again, and climbs to the famous long earthwork on Dodman Point called the Balk, Baulk or Bulwark **15**. This is an Iron Age earthwork on a grand scale. Two somewhat flattened Bronze Age barrows lie within the area. No dwelling sites have been found so far, but the remains of a medieval field system can be seen.

Having reached the top of the headland, the Coast Path now pleasantly contours the upper slopes to the tip of this noble promontory with its massive stone cross and well-preserved watch house **16**. Dodman Point, or the Dodman as it is usually called, is the most striking headland on the South Cornish

Hemmick Beach seen from the Coast Path, with Boswinger visible on the skyline.

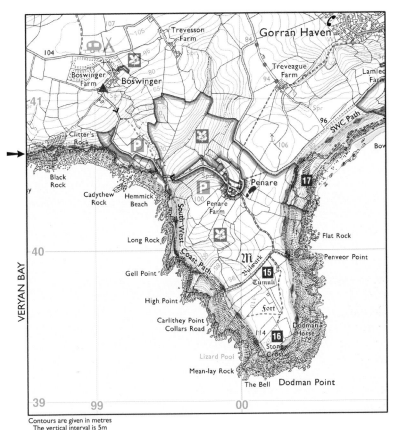

Contours are given in metres
The vertical interval is 5m

coast. Over the years it has caused numerous wrecks. The granite cross was built in 1896 by a local parson as a seamark, but unhappily it failed to save the destroyers *Thrasher* and *Lynx* from hitting rocks on the south-west side in fog a year later. A more recent tragedy was the pleasure boat *Darlwin*, which sank with all its passengers in 1966. A few yards inland from the Coast Path, and rather lost among the scrub, is a carefully preserved late-18th-century coastguard watch house, with its pulpit look-out alongside, and the only one of its kind on the Cornish coast.

From near the cross the path heads north along the east side of the Dodman, entering a large field by a stile, and then passing the east end of the earthwork mentioned above. The path carries on north, almost meeting the road at a place called The Gruda **17**, then slants along eastwards above the elegant parabola of Vault Beach. Hang-gliding is sometimes indulged in from The Gruda, which is a length of unfenced road.

41

Gorran Haven is near at hand, and a pleasant stroll round the rocky projection of Maenease Point soon brings the walker to this rapidly growing village. As you round Maenease Point, it is possible to take a detour along a path on the left, which takes you up amidst the crags to a plaque that remembers Sir John Fischer Williams of Lamledra, 'jurist and man of letters', who died in 1947.

The Coast Path reaches Gorran Haven **18** at Foxhole Lane. As you descend, note the terrace of old coastguard cottages on the opposite hillside, although the more recent extensive bungaloid growth may catch the eye to the exclusion of such features as Victorian buildings. Originally Porth Just, and later corrupted into Porth East, the place is the the 'haven' of Gorran, the parish centre situated 1 mile (1.6 km) inland. Fishing, and crabbing in particular, was the local calling, but, as a glance at the hillsides around the village will show, Gorran Haven is now a residential area for retired people and for those who work in St Austell.

To leave Gorran Haven, walk north up Church Street and turn into Cliff Road. Do not follow the signposted footpath near the bottom of Church Street. A right turn takes you to a stile at the end of Cliff Road. Along this stretch of path you may hear a bell-buoy tolling out to sea. At Great Perhaver, tunnels driven into the cliff were used to mine ochre, a material used in paint. An iron gantry was built as a loading quay for the ships that carried the mineral away at high tide.

Carn Rocks is a distinctive feature but the site shown on the map as 'earthwork' barely shows above ground level. Around the next headland, Turbot Point, is a small piece of cliff land, owned by the National Trust, and called Bodrugan's Leap **19**. Tradition states that here Sir Henry Trenowth of nearby Bodrugan, pursued by his enemy Sir Richard Edgcumbe of Cotehele, leapt into the sea and a waiting boat to escape to France during the reign of Henry VII.

Chapel Point now catches the eye, not for its natural appearance, but because of the three striking houses which were designed by John A. Campbell and built between 1933 and 1938 of stone taken from the site.

The Coast Path cuts across the neck of Chapel Point and carries on to rejoin the cliff top before briefly entering a small scrubby wood, then follows the Chapel Point track, which leads to the road south of Portmellon. Now a part of Mevagissey, this was formerly a boat-building and fishing centre. In 1849 many Mevagissey people fled to Portmellon during a cholera epidemic, and were accommodated in tents on the north side of the bay. From time to time the road is inundated by the sea.

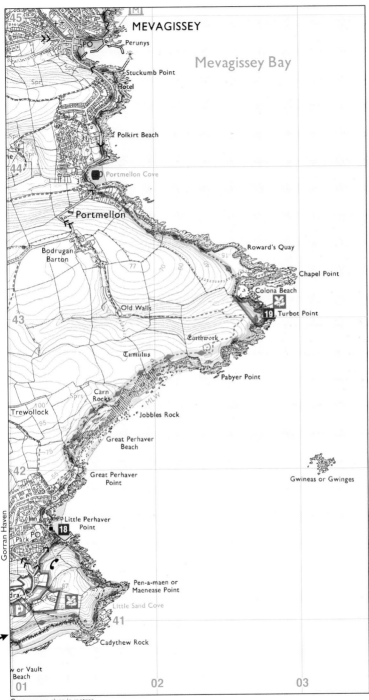

MEVAGISSEY

Mevagissey Bay

Perunys

Stuckumb Point

Hotel

Polkirt Beach

Portmellon Cove

Portmellon

Bodrugan
Barton

Roward's Quay

Chapel Point

Colona Beach

Old Walls

19 Turbot Point

43

Earthwork

Tumulus

Pabyer Point

Carn
Rocks

Trewollock

Jobbles Rock

Great Perhaver
Beach

42

Gwineas or Gwinges

Great Perhaver
Point

Gorran Haven

Inn

Little Perhaver
Point

Car
Park PO

18

Pen-a-maen or
Maenease Point

Little Sand Cove

dra

P

41

Cadythew Rock

w or Vault
Beach

01

02

03

Contours are given in metres
The vertical interval is 5m

43

Now take the road to Mevagissey; the two places are really one built-up area. As you walk into Mevagissey you can get off the road by passing through a small park overlooking the harbour. This sheltered fishing town repays a leisurely stroll around its back streets and waterfront, and a visit to the museum is strongly recommended. The first pier was built in 1430, but Mevagissey began to assume its present appearance in the late 18th century when the inner harbour was built. The outer harbour is only about a hundred years old.

As you leave Mevagissey heading north you pass the site of a Napoleonic War gun battery; the guns are now used as mooring bollards on the quays. Just above was one of Mevagissey's two ropewalks, where ropes were made for the local ships.

To leave the town, climb steeply up behind the toilets on the north side of the inner harbour, past the coastguard station. The Coast Path crosses a public open space, and you make for the eastern end of a terrace facing you.

After a series of ups and downs you will see ahead of you the massed ranks of caravans at Pentewan, and across the bay is the reptilian hump of Black Head. At deserted Portgiskey you can still see the remains of pilchard cellars amidst the undergrowth.

Once past Portgiskey the Coast Path follows a bank beside and above the B3273, and hugs it closely to join the road at the

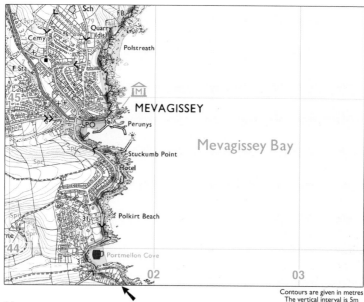

Contours are given in metres
The vertical interval is 5m

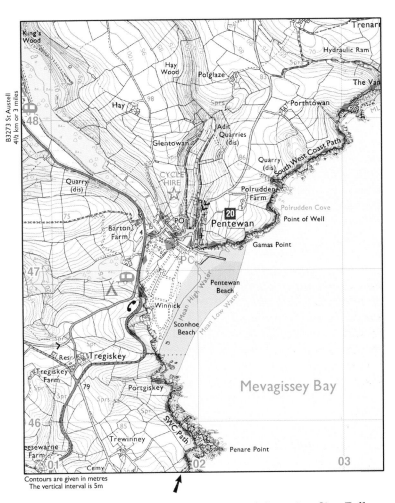

Contours are given in metres
The vertical interval is 5m

entrance to Pentewan Sands Caravan and Camping Site. Follow the road, leaving it where it is signposted Pentewan and going along West End. Part of the National Cycle Network can be joined here, running up the Pentewan Valley towards St Austell. Pentewan **20** is an interesting place as it is an artificial harbour (see page 49).

From the square, walk up Pentewan Hill for 100 yards (90 metres), and turn right along the Terrace. This is a pleasant, unspoilt row of houses with a church at the far end. Beyond the church, a signpost indicates the way to go. The Coast Path climbs between fences, and passes a concrete Second World War gun emplacement on the seaward side, from where there is an excellent view of the now blocked harbour outlet to the sea.

At The Vans, a wooded area, the Coast Path descends to a stream and meets another path coming from inland which leads to Hallane Mill Beach. The path goes behind a cottage and turns left then right before ascending towards Black Head.

Black Head is a distinctive promontory that has been in view for many miles past. This was bought by the National Trust in 1986. It was turned into a cliff castle in Iron Age times by the simple means of banking and ditching the isthmus. At a memorial to the Cornish writer A.L. Rowse, a path goes out to the top of Black Head, but the walker pressed for time can bypass this bonus by turning north and following the fenced-off path towards Trenarren. At the foot of the wooded cliff slope is another one-time pilchard station, Ropehaven **21**, not accessible by a public right of way.

Outside Trenarren House there is a small parking area, and at the north end a stile gives access to the next section of the Coast Path. Despite being so close to St Austell, this is a quiet and very rural part of the coast. Features to note are the place name Silvermine Point, and a rock arch to the north of Phoebe's Point. And then, suddenly, you are free-wheeling down to Porth Pean or Porthpean. The name means 'little harbour', in contrast to the 'great harbour' of Polmear, the Cornish name for Charlestown, three-quarters of a mile (1.2 km) to the north-east.

The Coast Path climbs steep steps at the north end of the beach and passes a two-storey Second World War lookout. A public open space is crossed, and then a route is followed above Du Porth Cliffs. You are now nearly at Charlestown. Pass beside the 19th-century sea defences and descend to the harbour.

What we now call Charlestown **22** began life as West Polmear (or Porthmeor), but it was then simply a small cove. In 1790 the population numbered nine, by 1801 it was 281 and 50 years later nearly 3,000 people lived in the newly built village. The place was now Charlestown, after Charles Rashleigh, the local mining entrepreneur who had invested his capital in creating this harbour to serve the St Austell china clay industry and the copper mines. Around the lockgated harbour, which was excavated out of the solid rock, Rashleigh established other industries: lime-burning, shipbuilding, brickmaking, net and bark houses, a rope walk and pilchard cellars.

Anyone with time to spare will find a visit to Charlestown visitor centre and Shipwreck Museum a fascinating experience.

AUSTELL
Sch
Cemetery
Long Stone
Cemetery Shaft (dis)
Sch
52
Superstore
22
Charlestown
PO
Shaft (dis)
Disused Workings
Gewans Farm
Mine (disused)
8
Lock
Duporth
Caravan Park
Shaft (dis)
Docks
Appletree Point
Tregorrick Road
Polmear Island
Quarry (dis)
Rugby Football Ground
Hospital
Duporth Holiday Village
Du Porth
51
86
Quarry (dis)
P
41
Carrickowel Point
H Ram Spr
52
Lower Porthpean
Porth Pean
Park Mathews Wood
CH
Robin's Rock
Higher Porthpean
Reservoir Outdoor Education Centre
Flat Rock
50
Penrice
Phoebe's Point
Castle Gotha
Castle Gotha
Silvermine Point
Lobb's Shop
Reservoir
107
Gwendra Point
104
49
P
Ropehaven
21
Trevissick
Gerrans Point
Ledrah
84
Trenarren
Hydraulic Ram
70
Polglaze
Hallane
The Bite
03
The Vans
04
Porthtowan
MLW
Fort
48
Adit Quarries (dis)
St Path
Drennick
Black Head

ST AUSTELL BAY

A CIRCULAR WALK ROUND DODMAN POINT

2 miles (3.2 km), with a possible extension of 2¹/₄ miles (3.6 km)

From the National Trust car park in the tucked-away hamlet of Penare, at the base of Dodman Point, or the Dodman, walk south along the farm track, turning right at the earthwork. When you reach the Coast Path, follow it round to the point and continue round, now heading north, past the eastern end of the earthwork, to The Gruda **17**, the unfenced road overlooking Vault Beach. Get up on to the road, turn left, go round the corner and, by a gate, climb the stile left, and cross the field to Penare and the car park.

This walk can be extended by 2¹/₄ miles (3.6 km) by carrying on east instead of joining the road at The Gruda. Then go round Maenease Point to Gorran Haven (see page 42), before returning along the road to The Gruda **17**, round the corner, then over the stile and across the field back to the car park.

Scale approx I inch to ¹/₂ mile

Contours are given in metres
The vertical interval is 5m

48

Pentewan

Pentewan **20** is the first of South Cornwall's three planned harbours you see as you walk from west to east; the others are Charlestown and Par. While the village is pleasant and well cared for, the harbour appears neglected by comparison. Its demise is largely the result of the sea choking the channel with sand.

The earliest harbour was built here in 1744 by the Hawkins family, but the present basin, quays and outlet to the sea were begun in 1820. Throughout its life the harbour was troubled by sand build-up and by china clay silt coming down the St Austell River, so the trade responsible for the port was largely responsible for its closure. The last china clay cargo left Pentewan in 1929, but shipments of sand continued outwards, with timber, coal, fertiliser and cement coming in. The railway was taken up in the First World War; the disused line is now part of the National Cycle Route. Later cargoes were removed from Pentewan by road.

Pentewan was the source of Pentewan stone, a hard, fine-grained stone much used in the local buildings and wharves, and employed in local churches as an interior and exterior material. One quarry, marked 'disused' on the map, will be seen beside the Coast Path on the way to Black Head.

Pilchard fishing

Seasonal pilchard fishing was carried on by the Cornish for hundreds of years until the shoals began to disappear in the 19th century. The fish were processed in fish cellars, and almost every inlet, and certainly every port, had its fishery. In the cellars the fish were packed in layers with salt and pressed to extract the oil. The square-cut holes in the side of cellar buildings were to receive one end of the timber press. The other end was weighted with a rock. After three or four weeks of pressing, the fish were packed into barrels for export. This trade gave employment to many, but the pervasive smell kept visitors at bay.

3 Charlestown to Fowey

through Polkerris and around the Gribbin
10 miles (16.1 km)

The china clay industry that created Charlestown **22** features heavily in this next stretch of the Coast Path. As well as the docks here, there are extensive works at Par, and at Fowey you may get a glimpse of the clay boats moored upstream. To pick up the Coast Path east of Charlestown, go around the harbour using the road. There is no right of way across the lockgate. The outer harbour is very attractive, with aesthetically satisfying granite bollards and steps.

Walk up the cliff path towards the toilets, noticing the line of square holes between granite blocks in the outer wall of the building on your left (north), used for pilchard pressing.

Pass through a kissing gate into a field and follow the fenced path around the edge of the fields to the fourth kissing gate. Now carry on along the path until it emerges on a road opposite the Porth Avallen Hotel. Follow the road for 80 yards (75 metres), and turn right (south-east).

The Coast Path follows the cliff edge and is confined. Where it meets a manicured open space, the path goes to the far end and passes in front of the large Carlyon Bay Hotel. Here you keep a fence to your left (north) and an open space to your right (south). Descend to a car park, pass down its seaward side and cross the road.

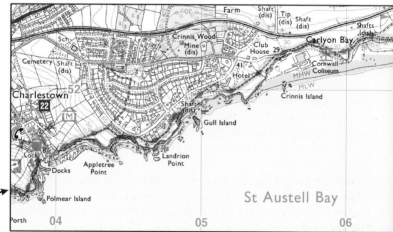

Contours are given in
The vertical interval

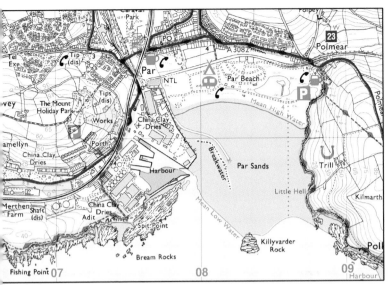

urs are given in metres
ertical interval is 5m

The route now runs along the top of the cliffs, with the Carlyon Bay Hotel Golf Club on the left (north), and the main railway line between London and Penzance just beyond. As you proceed east, the building and beach below you are the former Cornwall Coliseum, 'entertainment capital of the South West' in the 1980s. At the time of writing (2002) there are plans to redevelop the whole site into a luxury holiday complex.

The path gradually drops to Spit Point at the far end of the golf course. Ahead are the chimneys and paraphernalia of the china clay works, and the view beyond is of the pleasant unspoilt coastline between Polmear and the Gribbin, with the tiny village of Polkerris punctuating the cliffs. At Spit Point the path turns inland along a narrow double-fenced tarmac path which passes through the works.

After following the path with the railway line on your left, you come out on to the A3082 near the entrance to the clay works (see page 55). Turn right and follow the road, passing under a bridge, then turn right and cross the railway line at a level crossing. Now carry on along the pavement through a residential part of Par.

Stay on the pavement as you first turn right and then gently climb to walk behind the Par Beach Caravan Site. This brings you to Polmear, where the Coast Path goes up to the left of the Ship Inn; the well-restored Rashleigh Cottages **23** are on your far left.

For a short stretch as you climb uphill, you are walking along the Saint's Way **24**. This modern reconstruction of a possible Dark Age (AD 400–700) route between Fowey and Padstow imaginatively suggests that Celtic clerics and merchants travelled this way in preference to the sea journey around Land's End. A locally produced guidebook describes the route. After about 200 yards (180 metres), climb a wall on your right. The Coast Path now follows the cliff edge to Polkerris. On the first bit of this stretch there are two ways down from the path, to the car park and to the beach at low-tide mark.

The Coast Path descends narrrowly to the car park of the Rashleigh Inn at Polkerris **25**, which is one of Cornwall's most perfect fishing villages. Tucked into the bottom of a narrow valley, Polkerris has been saved from modern development by benign ownership. A pub, a café (in season) which occupies the old lifeboat house, and a straggle of cottages behind make up the village. But the castle-like pilchard cellars above the harbour, now neglected, were the *raison d'être* for Polkerris.

When you reach the beach, the Coast Path ascends from the slip to your left. It zigzags steeply through garlic-smelling sycamore woods and, reaching the top above the harbour, turns sharp right, giving a good view of the setting of Polkerris.

There now follows $1^{1}/_{2}$ miles (2.4 km) of easily traced Coast Path all the way to Gribbin Head **26**. A loop path descends in front of the Daymark, but the true route is to proceed north-east and take the path leading down to Polridmouth **27**, which is visible half a mile (800 metres) away.

The 84-foot (26-metre) red and white candy-striped Daymark was built in 1832 by Trinity House (the lighthouse and lightship authority) to enable sailors to distinguish the Gribbin from other South Cornish headlands. Unusually for Cornwall, the Gribbin bears much woodland, a mixture of sycamore, holly, beech and *Rhododendron ponticum*. The sea buckthorn, a prickly shrub with orange berries in the autumn, grows on the western side.

Polridmouth **27**, or Pridmth, has two sandy coves separated by a low bluff. The second (easterly) one has a lake behind it, and you must cross to the wooded slope beyond by the dam. Those who are not walking the Coast Path can easily reach Polridmouth down a farm track from a car park at Menabilly Barton. The beach house behind the easterly cove is the original dwelling that gave Daphne du Maurier the inspiration for *Rebecca*. 'Manderley' is really Menabilly, up the valley, where the author lived for many years.

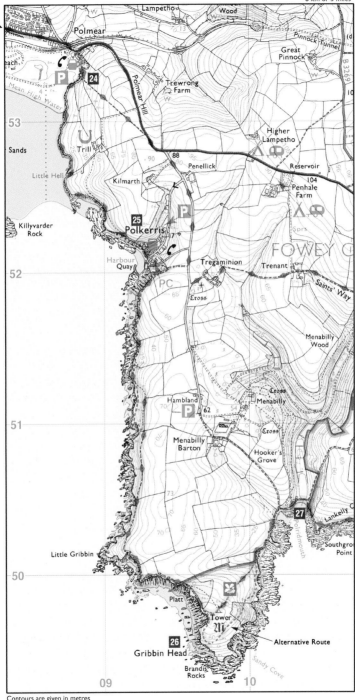

Lampetho
Wood

Polmear

Pinnock Tunnel

Great
Pinnock

B3369

Trewrong
Farm

Polmear Hill

24

P

Beach

Mean High Water

53

Sands

Trill

Little Hell

88

Penellick

Higher
Lampetho

Reservoir

104
Penhale
Farm

90

Kilmarth

Killyvarder
Rock

25

Polkerris

P

FOWEY

Harbour
Quay

Tregaminion

Trenant

Saints' Way

52

PC

Cross

Menabilly
Wood

Cross

Menabilly

Hambland

P

62

54

Cross

51

Menabilly
Barton

Hooker's
Grove

73

27

70

Lankelly

Little Gribbin

Polridmouth

Southgro
Point

50

Platt

Tower

Alternative Route

26

Gribbin Head

Brandis
Rocks

Sandy Cove

09

10

Contours are given in metres
The vertical interval is 5m

53

Turning right, up past the Lankelly Cliff omega sign, the Coast Path comes up out of woodland and passes two small coves where access to the beach is possible before Fowey is reached. The second is Coombe Haven (or Hawne). The path passes through Allday's Fields, given to Fowey in 1951, then enters woods to drop down to Readymoney Cove. You may wish to turn right (east) and follow a small path down and around to see St Catherine's Castle **28**, then return to the Coast Path.

The castle was built in 1540 by Thomas Treffry as one of the defences planned by Henry VIII along the south coast. It is now owned by English Heritage. The strange stone coronet inside protective railings above the castle is the Rashleigh Mausoleum, resting place of William Rashleigh, his wife and daughter.

The main path descends through Covington Woods, then turns right (east) at the bottom where Love Lane begins. There is another Saints' Way waymark here. From Readymoney Cove it is a simple walk into Fowey (pronounced 'Foy') and the foot ferry to Polruan.

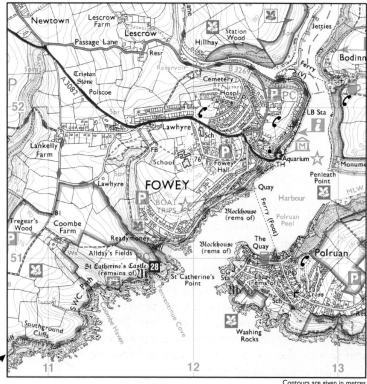

Contours are given in metres
The vertical interval is 5m

Par china clay works and harbour

Devon and Cornwall have the total UK reserves of this useful white mineral – china clay – whose extraction so strikes the northern visitor used to coal tips and slag heaps.

Apart from its use in the ceramic industry – china, porcelain, tiles, and sanitary ware – china clay is also used in the manufacture of paper, and the pages of this book contain a proportion of it, as a filler and whitener. Cosmetics, paint, rubber, crayons and many other commodities requiring a chemically inert filler use this rare mineral.

Par harbour was begun by J.T. Treffry – yet another of the Cornish industrialists who changed the face of early-19th-century Cornwall – but 20th-century expansion has totally changed its appearance. It is, of course, a shallow harbour and while it can accommodate more ships than Fowey, the latter benefits from a deep-water harbour at all states of the tide.

Fowey

Fowey enjoys the kind of situation at the mouth of a deep-water inlet that you will see again further east at Salcombe and Dartmouth.

The centre of the town is just below the fine church, which boasts a clerestory, a rare feature in Cornish churches. Here the life of the town pulsates, and there are pubs, restaurants and hotels. Near the church is Place, the family home of the Treffry family for over 500 years.

History tells us that Fowey was the focus of a rough and tumble in 1457 when the French landed and set fire to the port. Fowey men had long been aggressive marauding sailors, adopting a corsair-like approach to their private wars with France, so it was hardly surprising that the French decided on revenge. It failed to have any effect.

In 1469 John Willcock, a local captain, captured fifteen ships off the Brittany coast in a fortnight. This lawlessness embarrassed Edward IV, as he had just made peace with the French, so he sent a messenger to Fowey to tell the inhabitants to desist. The hapless emissary was sent back minus an ear.

Fowey is still a port, and large ships laden with china clay depart from wharves north of the town to destinations all over the world. There is a youth hostel at Penquite, Golant, about $3^1/_2$ miles (5.6 km) north of Fowey.

Looking down Polruan's narrow main street to Fowey.

4 Polruan to Looe

passing through Polperro
12 miles (19.3 km)

This is one of the finest stretches of walking between Falmouth and Exmouth. Having crossed by the foot ferry from Fowey (see page 158), it is worth having a look at Polruan before setting off. Polruan is to Fowey what Kingswear is to Dartmouth (see page 119). In the early 21st century both are smaller versions of their twins across the water, but it is likely that Polruan has a more ancient history than Fowey.

From the quay walk up the short hill to the foot of the steep main street, then turn sharp right along West Street. Now turn up Battery Lane, past the coastguard station, and on to an open space where there is a coastguard lookout. From here there are fine views westwards of the coast to Gribbin Head and the Dodman.

Where a fork occurs in the path, take the higher (inland) one, as the lower path goes down only to the Washing Rocks. The Coast Path passes a large, old vertical wall on the highest point by a less ancient watch house. This is all that remains of St Saviour's Chapel, probably built as a seamark.

Walk east through the village car park approach, then bear right down a signposted lane to the coastal fields. The path is now clear and Polruan is left behind.

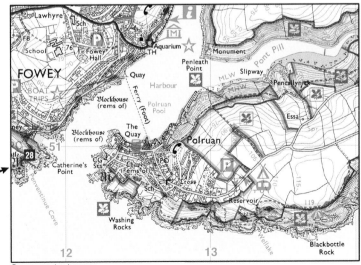

Contours are given in metres
The vertical interval is 5m

The Coast Path climbs, and enters National Trust land at Blackbottle Rock (surely a smuggling reference!). Where the Coast Path enters Trust land note the dog stile devised by National Trust warden Leslie Hicks. A simple lifting device enables owners to pass their possibly elderly and probably muddy dogs through the barrier without having to lift them. At the highest point a seat is reached, a good place to take in the view of Pencarrow Head. Thrift grows here in season, and foxgloves line the path like a wedding guard of honour.

The path dips to pass round Lantic Bay, and a short link path heads inland by a National Trust moneybox to join the east-to-west hinterland road. It passes a now disused tip on which exotic plants are known to bloom. The Coast Path climbs steeply above Great Lantic Beach to meet another link path coming from the road and a strategically sited car park, then turns 90 degrees to the south with a high and a low option towards Pencarrow Head. A steep path cuts down the cliffside to the beach, where swimming can be dangerous because of strong currents and shelving sands.

To the east of Pencarrow Head, a satisfying promontory with some jutting rocky outcrops, the path passes behind a privately owned 19th-century watch house, best seen from the other side of Lantivet Bay, before turning due east. At this point another

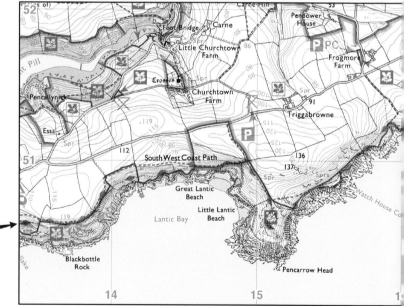

Contours are given in
The vertical interval

path goes inland to a large car park at Frogmore, which has the extra facility of toilets.

A scramble path descends to a low-tide cove west of Sandheap Point – Palace Cove – where there are the scant remains of a pilchard palace or cellar. The Coast Path then drops steeply to Lansallos Cove **29**, an unspoilt inlet that can also be reached by a delightful lane from Lansallos village. No sewage is discharged near this beach.

Local farmers of perhaps 200 years ago were responsible for the curious cutting at the back of this beautiful little bay. It enabled them to get their small carts and pack animals down to the beach to collect sand and seaweed for the land. A water mill stood nearby and disappeared only in the last 25 years or so.

To proceed east walk up the valley for 200 yards (180 metres) to a wicket gate, then turn right (south) along a track, entering a field briefly, to reach a stile built between stone posts.

The Coast Path now heads east with no route-finding problems for 2 miles (3.2 km), although there are severe gradients. The Lansallos National Trust land is left behind at East Coombe at a wooden footbridge, and from here a three-quarter-mile (1.2-km) National Trust permissive path goes up the valley to the road at Windsor Farm.

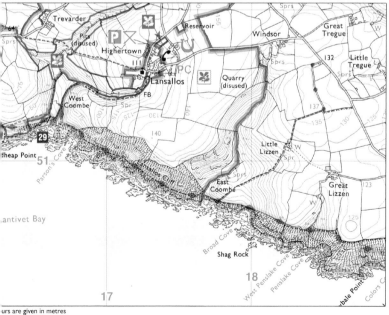

urs are given in metres
vertical interval is 5m

Beyond the stream a public right of way leaves the Coast Path and slants steeply north-east to the derelict building of Little Lizzen, used at one time by Marie Stopes, the pioneer of birth control, as a holiday cottage. The white Daymark beside the path lines up with a white mark lower down the cliff to warn boats of the Udder Rock out to sea. The Udder Rock bell-buoy may be heard tolling its solemn warning. The rock itself is exposed at very low tides.

From the Raphael Cliff National Trust sign a natural rock arch is visible at sea level. The next sign announces Chapel Cliff, pronounced 'Chaypel'. From here until Polperro there are several paths leading off the main track; do not take any of them unless you want to make life difficult for yourself. The land adjacent to the Coast Path on either side of the village was once used by the locals for growing flowers and vegetables; old gates mark the entrances to these now-overgrown plots.

As you near the mouth of Polperro harbour, the large shed standing in the lee of Peak Rock is the net loft, now owned by

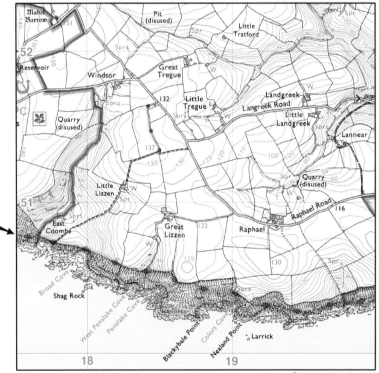

Contours are given in metres
The vertical interval is 5m

the National Trust but once the building where fishermen stored and maintained their nets. The path drops down to the harbour either on the seaward side of the Three Pilchards Inn or near the Blue Peter Café: it splits in two, but the destination is the same. Polperro is best seen when the tide is in and the waterfront houses seem to float on the water.

To leave Polperro, walk round the north side of the harbour, past a pleasant sitting-out area, and take the higher path at a fork. The lower path is Reuben's Walk, named after a local man, Reuben Oliver, who was Polperro's harbourmaster. A steep path comes down from Brent, an estate to the north, and there are more of those now-overgrown private cultivation plots beside the path. At the next fork stay low, taking care in wet weather on the rocky path. The shared War Memorial for Talland and Polperro is reached at Downend Point. Two pairs of black and white striped beacons (shown on the map as 'landmarks') to the east delineate a nautical measured mile for speed trials offshore.

Contours are given in metres
The vertical interval is 5m

The inner harbour at Polperro.

The path, much used by local walkers, carries on round into Talland Bay. After a stile and some steps, it drops steeply down to the beach, Talland Bay West, which is safe for bathing. Over the low headland, Talland Bay East is smaller. A short distance up the lane from here and worth visiting is Talland Church, which is chiefly remarkable for its detached tower and old bench-ends. Talland House was the inspirational home of the novelist Francis Brett-Young.

The Coast Path now strikes out to an unnamed promontory which the National Trust has designated Hendersick on its omega signs, after the nearby farm of that name. Along this stretch you may be aware for the first time of the Eddystone Lighthouse 14 miles (22.5 km) to the south-east.

Once at the tip of the point, St George's Island (or Looe Island) **30** comes into view ahead; the island is currently leased by the Cornwall Wildlife Trust. In the Middle Ages the island was always called after St Michael, but in the 17th century it began to be called St George's Island, perhaps in error! Now it is usually known as Looe Island.

From the headland a link path goes inland to the National Trust car park near Hendersick Farm. The Coast Path now hugs the coastline all the way to Hannafore, the first bit of built-up Looe that you reach. Above you are the remains of the Chapel of Lamanna, built by the monks of Glastonbury in the 1100s. Note

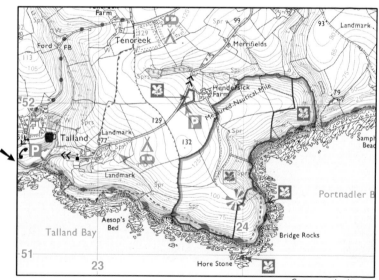

Contours are given in metres
The vertical interval is 5m

also the ancient wall forming the field boundary of the first house, significantly called Monks House. Two splayed windows and some square holes look enigmatically westwards.

Having reached the road, the bridge between West and East Looe is still 1 mile (1.6 km) away, but the walk is not hard. A grass strip beside the pavement helps ease tired muscles, and there are opportunities for refreshment and much to see, as boats pass in and out of the harbour. In the main holiday season a ferry shuttles pedestrians across the harbour, which can save a few hundred yards' walk to the bridge further north.

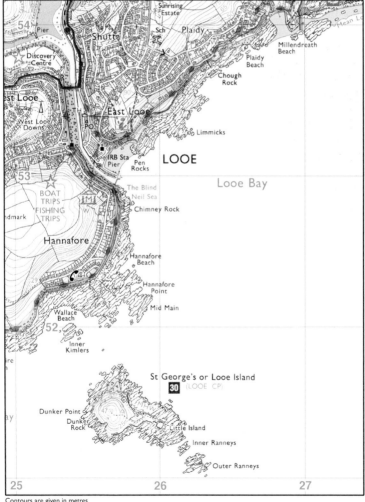

Contours are given in metres
The vertical interval is 5m

5 Looe to Cremyll

via Portwrinkle and Mount Edgcumbe Country Park
21 miles (33.8 km)

This is a lengthy section of the Coast Path. After leaving Looe and its eastward extensions, good stretches along high cliffs take you to Rame Head, where you turn inland and end with a stroll through a country park.

After crossing the bridge at Looe the Coast Path goes right, down the main street and into the centre of the town. When you get to the Salutation Inn, turn left up Castle Street to an open area at the top overlooking the beach. Alternatively, carry on past the inn and take the next left. This road takes you out to the seafront, passing en route the town's museum, housed in the old Guildhall. This is well worth a visit. The Coast Path can then be reached by a zigzag path and steps from the sea wall behind East Looe Beach.

The Coast Path leaving Looe is mainly on tarmac. When a road is reached, turn down Plaidy Lane. In the spring or early summer, you will have a good view of fulmars perched on an outcrop to the right (south) as you descend.

Plaidy Beach is a small shingle strand with a modern sea wall behind it. The road, along which the Coast Path is routed, leads eastwards with houses on both sides. The path turns sharp right, up a steep, signposted, tarmac path, opposite a house with a steeply pitched roof. It passes through a small parking area, along a level road and, where this bends left, the Coast Path descends between two houses at a waymarked junction. The path leads down to Millendreath and emerges from behind an entertainment complex. The valley is totally given over to holiday enjoyment.

From the east end of Millendreath Beach the Coast Path is signposted up a lane past a number of houses. This is an attractive lane of the kind which must have served countless Cornish coves 100 years ago. This one has never been 'improved'.

When the path reaches a tarmac road at Bodigga **31** look out for a gate on the right (south) side after about 150 yards (135 metres). A National Trust omega sign reads 'Bodigga Cliff'. Now you leave the road for about 1½ miles (2.4 km), and after descending rough land the path enters woods through which it undulates for some distance. Two minor paths, one up and one down, should be ignored, but the Coast Path is unmistakeable.

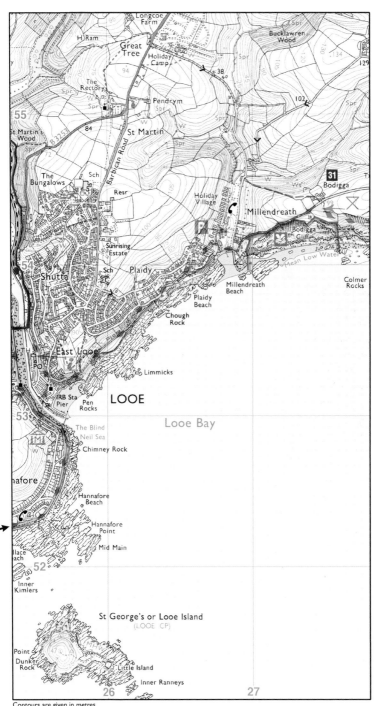

Contours are given in metres
The vertical interval is 5m

Emerging from the woodland, the path goes across an open stretch of scrubby land before descending to the road west of Seaton, down a flight of steps. Be careful on the road as there is no pavement. At Seaton you will find the Seaton Valley Countryside Park and local nature reserve. The river rises high on Bodmin Moor and it is possible to follow a path all the way along the riverside to the village of Hessenford $1^1/_2$ miles (2.5 km) upstream. Part of the walk is suitable for disabled people and a picnic area gives good views of the valley.

Eastwards from here there is a choice. The official Coast Path follows the road up towards Downderry, a stretched-out village about a mile long, with modern houses at the east end. The older core is pleasant enough, and here there are shops, pubs, cafés and a post office. This is a busy, narrow road and care should be taken at all times. Alternatively, you can walk along the beach if the tide is out, returning to the road at the east end of

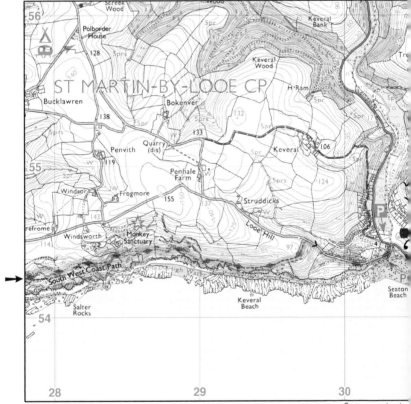

Contours are given in r
The vertical interval i

Downderry, by a school, garage and church **A**. On the beach you may see the distinctive inshore crabbers drawn up. They have a small mizzen mast offset to the port side.

Perhaps surprisingly, the highest points on the south coast of Cornwall are on either side of Downderry. To the east, the Coast Path ascends to Battern Cliffs (462 feet/141 metres). To the west, although the path does not climb that far, the road between Seaton and Bodigga reaches 508 feet (155 metres).

Continue along the road to a point round the first hairpin bend where the Coast Path is signposted to the right. The path is steep in places and zigzags about, but is well cared for.

A new stretch of the Coast Path forks off to the right just before a stile is reached, thus avoiding the stretch of road to Portwrinkle. This follows the cliff edge between a fence on the left and occasional stretches of wall on the seaward side. It soon passes, on the right, the ruins of St Germans Hut, so covered in

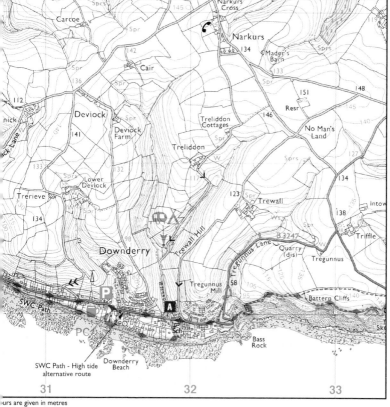

greenery that it is hard to make out. This was built for the Earls of St Germans as a shooting lodge, later becoming a teashop. Above it in the field stands a barrow (Bronze Age grave), also overgrown.

The Long Stone soon comes into view on the approach to Cargloth Cliffs and this is a good place to spot sea birds. The path continues towards Portwrinkle, passing below a bungalow and on to Britain Point. Here care should be taken, as the path is very close to the cliff edge and is unfenced.

Just before reaching Portwrinkle you pass a white-painted stone plinth in which fires were lit to guide boats back into the harbour after dark. The path now goes between some gardens at the back of a row of cottages and joins a lane, where you turn right down to the harbour.

Portwrinkle **32** possesses a charm that is lacking in Seaton and Downderry, but the broad sweep of Whitsand Bay tends to overpower the settlements along its shores. The village came into existence as a pilchard fishery, and the large (for such a small place) cellars stand at the top of the slip above the harbour.

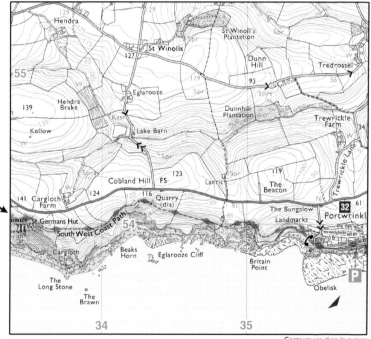

Contours are given in metres
The vertical interval is 5m

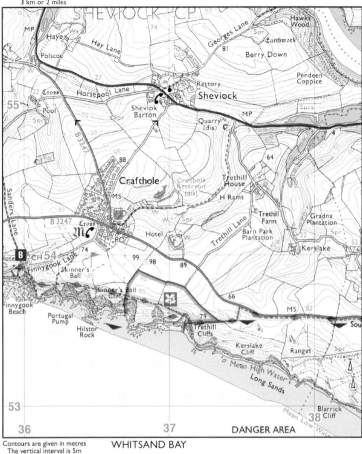

A374 Polbathic
3 km or 2 miles

SHEVIOCK CP

Contours are given in metres
The vertical interval is 5m

WHITSAND BAY

DANGER AREA

Walk east along the road from Portwrinkle harbour past the car park, ignoring a path down to the beach. The Coast Path leaves the road opposite the main entrance to the Whitsand Bay Hotel **B**. This imposing building was rebuilt here in 1911, having formerly been Thanckes Manor at Torpoint. Originally built in 1871, it was taken down in 1909 and moved here by Sir Reginald Pole Carew, the local landowner.

The narrow path climbs steeply to the golf course. It follows an obvious route along the edge of the links, confirmed by the occasional signpost. A footpath leads off to the left across the course to the village of Crafthole, where there is a shop, inn and post office. Soon the Coast Path reaches National Trust land at Trethill Cliffs, and after a level stretch it dips steeply and climbs towards the top black-and-white pole. The Tregantle firing ranges are

71

nearby, and signs warn of the dangers. At the time of writing, work is underway to create a permissive path through the ranges. This will be available to the public on days when firing is not taking place. Please be guided by the signs and information.

If the ranges are in use, climb a stile, follow the field edge and then join the road at the eastern end of Trethill Cliffs. From this point for 4 miles (6.4 km) the Coast Path follows the road, although this is not as bad as it sounds. For about half a mile (800 metres) the path is over the hedge from the road, and it is then possible to walk on a wide grass verge where it goes inland round Tregantle Fort **33**. This massive structure is one of around 40 forts and batteries built in the 1860s and early 1870s to protect Plymouth from newly developed French sea power.

Just past the entrance to Tregantle Fort the road returns to the coast at Tregantle Down, and here a path gives access to the

Contours are given in metres
The vertical interval is 5m

72

Looking east to Rame Head along Whitsand Bay from Sharrow Point.

beach, which can be used when firing is not taking place. The stretch of land called Tregantle Cliffs is protected by the National Trust, and a path has been cut along this rough land so that walkers can avoid the road.

Nearly at Freathy there is a large car park to the north of the road, and a sign on the south of the road indicates Sharrow Point. A path goes down here to Sharrow Grotto **34**, almost at sea level, and a short digression is worth the effort involved to

73

take it. The Grotto is an artificial cave, hacked out of the cliff by a naval lieutenant called Lugger in 1784 as a therapy for his gout.

East of here there is a change of land ownership and Freathy is reached. For the next 2 miles (3.2 km), the Military Road **35** passes above a cliff peppered with huts, shacks and chalets dating back to the early 1930s. There are occasional seasonal cafés, but no opportunity to leave the road until the turning to Whitsand Bay Holiday Park is reached **C**.

At the Holiday Park junction **C**, where there is a postbox, a path goes down to the Clifftop Café. Do not take this path. Instead, take the path slanting down the cliff slope on a line with the pyramid of Rame Head. This is signposted and there are waymark posts along the route, past a small community of about ten huts in a combe on the cliffs.

From here a path descends to the beach, but the Coast Path climbs steeply towards the road. When about 5 yards (4.5 metres) short of the road, turn off right (south) and follow this further loop path, just east of Rame View Café. The Coast Path is signposted and waymark posts are in position along the route.

Not far down, you pass a seat dedicated to Bill Best Harris, one-time Plymouth City Librarian, broadcaster and local author 'who loved these cliffs'. Just past his seat, turn up left, ignoring the path to the beach. The Coast Path undulates along and almost reaches the road near the junction to Wiggle. It then descends once more, bearing left and leaving the huts behind, passes a shuttered lean-to building, belonging to Plymouth YMCA, and crosses a stile. The path now goes across rough ground to a private drive. Turn right, passing behind the row of old coastguard cottages, and go up a flight of steps. The path goes round the tennis court of the former Polrawn Fort **36**, now converted into flats below.

The way ahead is now clear, and this is the beginning of a circuit of Rame Head. The walking is easy, and soon there is a hedge (in Cornwall a hedge is a wall!) which displays a fine variety of plants in the summer. Steps lead up to a rocky outcrop. Rame Head is now quite close and is definitely worth a visit.

No walker should be surprised to find the obligatory ditch and bank across the narrow isthmus, making Rame Head defensible in Iron Age times. Practically every similar headland in Devon and Cornwall was so used. The sturdy chapel has embellished Rame Head for about 600 years, and has thus lasted far beyond the temporary structures which were raised for hostilities only during the two World Wars.

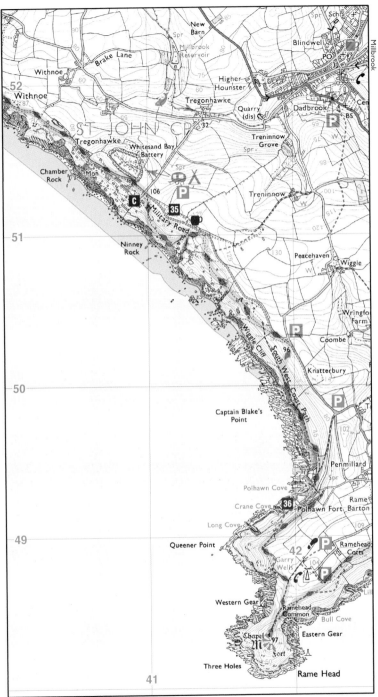

Contours are given in metres
The vertical interval is 5m

From the neck of Rame Head, ignore a lower path and follow the signposted route ascending to a wall corner. At Homebarton Hill a link path crosses a field to Rame Church, and half a mile (800 metres) further on another link path goes up to a car park on the site of the one-time Penlee Battery. When the path reaches a tarmac loop, take the lower option, which leads to a turning area and seats at Penlee Point **37**, where the Coast Path turns north and joins the Earl's Drive through sycamore woodland. Just after a quarry left and a seat right, bear downhill along a signposted path. This emerges on a road again behind the coastguard cottages, then continues to contour while the road climbs. The way ahead to Cawsand is now clear, and the Coast Path descends into the village by Pier Lane. Cawsand and Kingsand have coalesced into one place, although they retain their separate identities.

These twin villages represent the archetypal Cornish coastal settlement. Until 1844, Kingsand was in Devon and Cawsand in Cornwall, an anomalous situation which led to rivalry. In the summer it is possible to reach Plymouth quickly from Cawsand by catching one of the regular sailings from the beach to Mayflower Steps, but this would mean missing the scenic delights of Mount Edgcumbe Country Park. Cawsand is linked to Kingsand by Garrett Street, a narrow lane passable by vehicles

The Square, Cawsand, with the fountain in the foreground.

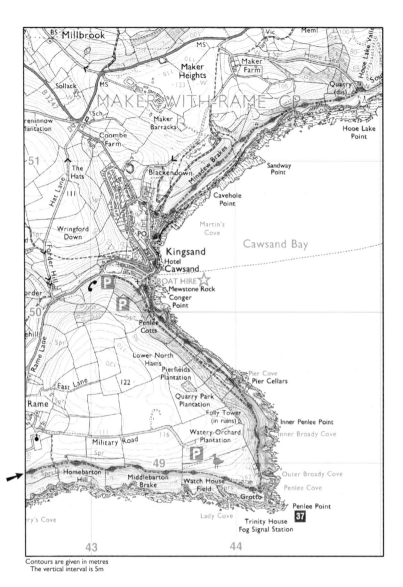

Contours are given in metres
The vertical interval is 5m

only from north to south, and once in Kingsand the way out of
the village is to turn right into Market Street towards the clock
tower, then left into an open area where several lanes meet. Take
the right-hand lane, Heavitree Road. Opposite Lower Row turn
right into Mount Edgcumbe Country Park, here a recreational
area with a striking view of Plymouth Sound. The Coast Path
contours this field, then enters a wood of evergreen oaks called
Dark Trees.

At Hooe Lake the path meets the public road leading to Picklecombe Fort, now a complex of desirable apartments, and after 50 yards (45 metres) the route turns left and you pass through a kissing gate then walk uphill parallel to the road. When above the fort buildings the Coast Path turns through 90 degrees 'inland' – this is the Earl's Drive once again – and where it returns to the sea you will see a feature on the bend called Picklecombe Seat. The stonework for this late-18th-century conceit came from a church in Stonehouse, Plymouth.

Around the next bend, the path now diverts (due to a recent landslide) into a feature of the estate known as the Zigzag. The path winds upwards, reaching an old three-arched folly at the top before descending via some steps, across the Earl's Drive and down to the cliff edge. The path drops further to a pebble beach and crosses a wooden walkway. From here Drake's Island **38** appears very close. At low tide the reef known as the Bridge reaches out from the land and the island. The deep-water channel is on the east side of the island.

Beyond the beach, the path climbs through open woodland and exits a deer enclosure, so be sure to close the gate. At this spot look up left to see the ruin known simply as the Folly **39**. This is one of a number of landscape features built by the Mount Edgcumbe family to enliven their estate, and we are fortunate that this large area, so near to Plymouth, is now open to the public as a country park.

The path descends to the amphitheatre where a temple overlooks a lake with ducks, surrounded by lawns. Carrying on, you pass a boulder-built grotto, then a beach, Barn Pool, used as a tank embarkation site for the invasion of northern France in the Second World War. The path now reaches more formal gardens, with a 1540 fort on the left and a later battery on the right, complete with a mounted French 8-pounder cannon.

The Orangery, where refreshments are served, is reached, and the entrance/exit of the Country Park is situated nearby. The visitor centre is worth a visit and maybe, if time allows, you might look over Mount Edgcumbe House on the hill. Unfortunately the house, dating from 1540, was destroyed by fire in 1941, but the ruins were well restored. The estate, which takes in much of the coastline round to Whitsand Bay, became a country park in 1970. Leaflets and other publications are on sale in the visitor centre, and guided walks are undertaken by the Ranger Service.

The ferry leaves this point – Cremyll – for Stonehouse on the other side at fairly frequent intervals (see page 158).

Penlee Point

Penlee Point **37** is an important feature on the Coast Path, for here the path changes direction and Plymouth comes into view. The 1827 grotto just below the path is known as Adelaide's 'chapel', though it never had pretensions to sanctity. The Earl of Mount Edgcumbe had the Earl's Drive built out to Penlee Point – you come across it again in Mount Edgcumbe Country Park – and had the grotto built in honour of Princess Adelaide, the wife of Prince William (later King William IV) who stayed at Mount Edgcumbe and enjoyed visiting Penlee.

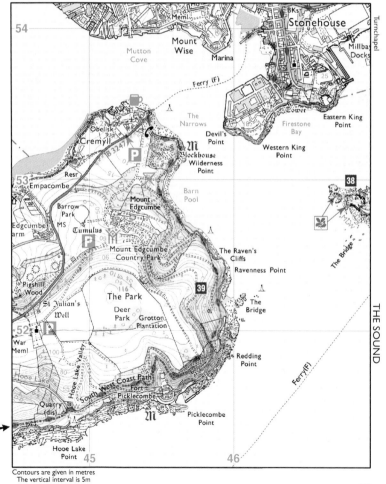

Contours are given in metres
The vertical interval is 5m

6 Stonehouse to Wonwell

through Plymouth, via Warren Point and along Revelstoke Drive
24 miles (38.6 km)

On disembarking from the ferry at Admirals Hard, you will notice the blue pillar on the left of the slip. This marks the start of the Plymouth Waterfront Walkway, stating it is 10 miles to Jennycliff and 352 to Minehead. This route was developed by Plymouth City Council and is the only stretch of the South West Coast Path to run through a city. Along the route, marked by acorns on white hoops painted on lampposts, you will come across sculptures, poetry, industrial relics as well as passing through some of Plymouth's most interesting areas. A copy of the booklet describing the walk can be obtained from the TIC at the Barbican, Plymouth (£2.50, p&p extra).

Along the way the path passes pubs and cafés such as those at Stonehouse. The pubs bear a plaque based on a token given to the workers on the Eddystone lighthouse in 1757. It stopped them being taken away by the press gangs. A knitted fried breakfast originally made for Elvira's Café has been turned into a plaque to mark the cafés.

Turn right in front of the Vine Hotel, then left at the quay, passing beside a playground, then right down Cremyll Street to

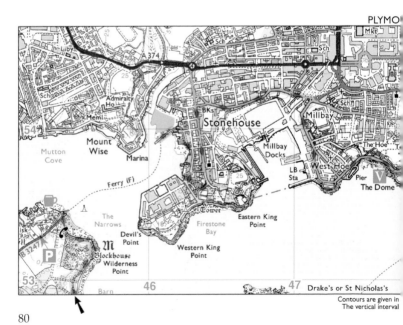

Contours are given in
The vertical interval

the Royal William Yard. This complex of buildings was built in the early 1800s to supply the Royal Navy with food and drink. It ceased to belong to the Navy in 1992, and there are plans to open the whole area to the public in the near future.

Passing between the yard wall and the pub, head out to the area overlooking Firestone Bay before turning left towards Durnford Street. Walk up this long street of fine Georgian houses until you reach the far end of Stonehouse Barracks, where the path turns right down Millbay Road. Follow the road to the roundabout outside Millbay Docks, where stars set into the wall tell of famous people who disembarked here in the past.

Head in the direction of the Duke of Cornwall Hotel, turning right at the next roundabout by the Eddystone Lighthouse pavement. The path follows West Hoe Road, overlooking the ferryport for France and Spain.

The octagonal building on your right is Plymouth Lifeboat Station, and just after this the Coast Path leaves the road and passes in front of the large houses beside the Rusty Anchor bus stop. This walkway offers great views out into the Sound, across to Drake's Island and Mount Edgcumbe beyond. As you round the point Plymouth Hoe comes into view, and the path now rejoins the road heading in that direction.

Contouring around the Hoe, below Smeaton's Lighthouse and the Dome (worth a visit to explore Plymouth's past), the

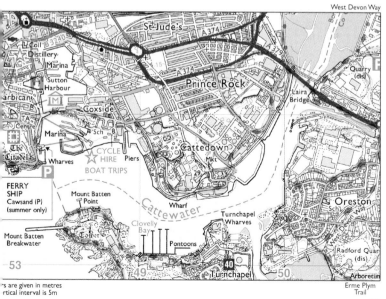

path keeps to the coast, turning right down Madeira Road. Above the road towers the Royal Citadel, built on the orders of Charles II in the years after 1665, and still a military barracks. The path now descends towards Sutton Harbour and the Mayflower Steps. Take some time to explore the Barbican, the old part of Plymouth, with its shops, cafés and art galleries.

The Coast Path crosses the entrance to Sutton Harbour by the swing bridge over to the National Marine Aquarium. Follow the trail of silver fish in the pavement, up past the aquarium and on to Teats Hill Road. Continue along Clovelly Road, with the gas tanks on the left, turning right on to Breakwater Hill, where a large red-and-white-striped navigation beacon 'points' the way forward. Traffic is now left behind as the Coast Path winds its way above the docks of the Cattewater to re-emerge in an area full of warehouses and factories. This is the industrial side of Plymouth – not the most picturesque area, but it was here at the mouth of the Plym that the city's name originated, and it was from here that Sir Francis Drake set off around the world in 1577.

Continue past the Passage House Inn, over the railway line and along Maxwell Road. At the roundabout turn right along Finnegan Road. The Coast Path now reaches the A379 at Laira Bridge. Turn right, cross the bridge and carry on up Billacombe Road to another roundabout. Turn right, crossing Breakwater Road, and head straight up the hill, turning right again. This next stretch of the route follows a very busy road with no pavement; take care.

Leave Oreston Road, turning right into Rollis Park Road, and descend to the quay. At the far end of the green turn right in front of Minards House, then left into Park Road. A red diamond sign sits at the top of the hill, where the path turns left and snakes between hedges, passing an allotment on your right.

The Coast Path then descends to Radford Lake, where it crosses a causeway and passes under the arch of Radford Castle. A metal stile is reached as the path winds along beside Hooe Lake, reaching another stile before entering Hexton Hill Road. Below, the wall of the Royal Oak Pub has a red diamond plaque on it pointing left and around Hooe Green. Here the Coast Path has to head inland, although it is hoped that a more coastal route will be open soon; you should therefore follow signs on the ground. The present route turns left, then right up Church Hill Road, passing the Church. Follow St John's Road as it descends past Fort Stamford to a car park at the bottom. In the far corner of the car park steps lead down to the waterline to pass between modern flats and the marina.

From the marina's car park, yellow hatch lines mark the route of the Coast Path as it crisscrosses its way between boats and cars. It then crosses the slipway of the Mountbatten Centre and follows the water around to the landing stage for the ferry from Sutton Harbour. The redeveloped Mountbatten area is close at hand with its bars and cafés, or you could take a few minutes to admire the views from the breakwater. The Coast Path itself ascends the cliff beside a white stone commemorating the flying boats that used to take off from here. The steps lead up to an

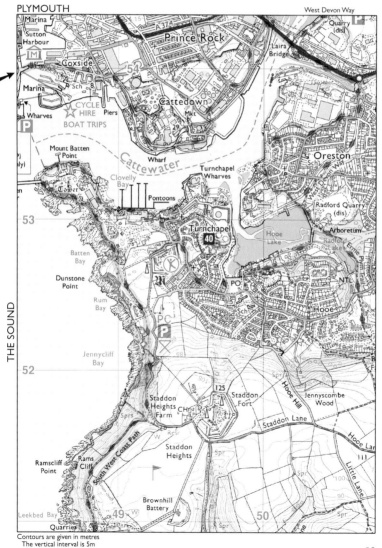

Contours are given in metres
The vertical interval is 5m

open area with the artillery tower at the far end, but the Coast Path descends again on the right. Head towards a beach, where a short stretch of road is used before the path passes in front of a large building now converted into expensive apartments.

The path climbs up behind Dunstone Point to reach Jennycliff, a spectacular and popular viewpoint. Walk across Jennycliff Field towards a white stone, then across another field to a blue pillar marking the end of the Waterfront Walkway. Go through a stile and follow the path as it weaves its way through woodland. Soon Plymouth Breakwater **41** comes into view, and on the inland side the enormous brick wall is the back stop of a firing range.

Fort Bovisand and harbour **42** lie just below. The harbour was built between 1816 and 1824, initially to enable ships to take on fresh water without having to go up to the dockyard. A reservoir was constructed in the valley behind Bovisand Bay, and the water piped to the ships.

The Coast Path descends steps behind Fort Bovisand, bears left, and crosses a deep ravine by a footbridge. This artificial cutting was excavated to enable ammunition and supplies to be transported to the fort below. A further drop **A** brings you down between two rows of cottages. Turn left and walk through the car park, taking the right fork leading down to the beach. The path passes behind Bovisand Bay and then climbs up to follow the road in front of the holiday complex.

Once past Andurn Point you can enjoy three-quarters of a mile (1.2 km) of pleasant easy rambling along low cliffs almost at sea level. Although only 2 miles (4 km) has been covered since leaving

Fort Bovisand, now a training school for underwater activities.

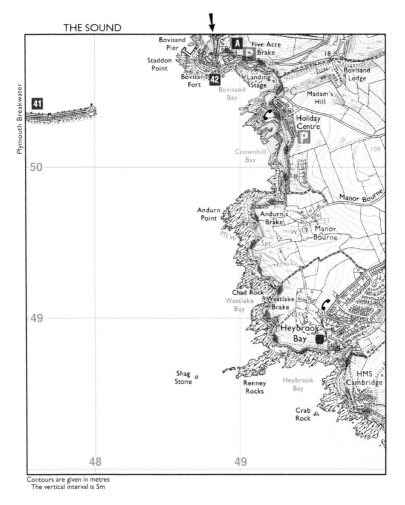

THE SOUND

Plymouth Breakwater

41

A
P
Bovisand Pier
Staddon Point
Bovisand Fort **42**
Bovisand Bay
Five Acre Brake
18
Landing Stage
Bovisand Lodge
Madam's Hill
Holiday Centre **P**
109
Crownhill Bay

50

Andurn Point
Andurn Brake
Manor Bourne
53
Manor Bourne
MLW
Spr

49

Chad Rock
Westlake Bay
Westlake Brake
Heybrook Bay

Shag Stone
Renney Rocks
Heybrook Bay
HMS Cambridge
Crab Rock

48
49

Contours are given in metres
The vertical interval is 5m

Turnchapel, several different types of rock have been traversed. Turnchapel is on Plymouth limestone, Jennycliff on tuffs, abreast of Staddon Heights there were grits and shales, and there is slate at Bovisand. South of Andurn Point the low cliffs bear deposits of head, a matrix of rock waste formed in Ice Age times by alternate freezing and thawing. This is a conglomerate material brought down from higher levels when colder conditions prevailed. The transition from one geological structure to another is a typical feature of the South Devon coast.

When you reach the long ridge of Renney Rocks, keep to the path along the cliff edge. This leads you into Heybrook Bay, a bit of Plymouth suburbia-by-the-sea. Until recently, Wembury Point, to the east, was the site of HMS *Cambridge*, the Royal

Navy gunnery school. Since the closure of HMS *Cambridge* in 2001, you are free to continue along the Coast Path in the knowledge that there will be no explosions!

As you pass HMS *Cambridge* you are as near the Great Mew Stone **43** as you will get. This is one of several similarly named rocks along the south coast – 'mew' being an old name for gull. In 1744 a man was sentenced to live on the rock for seven years as a punishment for petty crime.

The Coast Path to Wembury Beach is easily followed as it traces the low cliff edge. A one-time water mill is now a seasonal café run by the National Trust, and there is a National Trust shop nearby. In 1994 the Devon Wildlife Trust opened the Wembury Marine Centre as a result of a Voluntary Marine Conservation Area having been designated from Fort Bovisand to Gara Point. On the hill above the large car park is Wembury Church **44**, so conspicuously sited that it must have been built here as a land-mark for shipping. Wembury Beach is the starting point of the Erme–Plym Trail which, when used with the Two Moors Way, provides a link across Devon to the coast at Lynton.

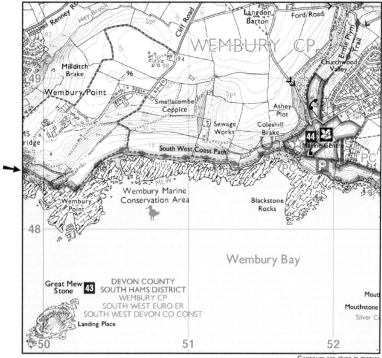

Contours are given in metres
The vertical interval is 5m

The Coast Path climbs eastwards from just behind the café, and in the summer a notice at the path take-off point informs walkers of the ferry times, as $1^1/_2$ miles (2.4 km) further on the River Yealm (pronounced 'Yam') has to be crossed, and the operating times of the ferry are limited (see page 158).

The path to the Yealm is a high-level one with fine views ahead. National Trust land is soon entered, and the path is mostly within Trust ownership until Stoke Point is reached 6 miles (9.6 km) on. At the Rocket House **B**, where coastguard apparatus used to be stored, the path descends down the vehicle track to the right. The descent is steep and brings you past cottages to the ferry point. Provided the ferry is running it can be hailed from here.

When you land on the Noss Mayo side, note the restored ferryman's sign exhibited there. Part of it reads: 'Ferriage for every person on weekdays 1d; the like on Sundays 2d. For every pony and ass 3d.'

Now turn right (west) along a narrow path that climbs through oak woods in which the invasive rhododendron is beginning to take hold. The path meets a wide drive just short of a gate where there is a National Trust interpretive panel. Beyond the gate the drive continues round a bend at Battery Cottage, a

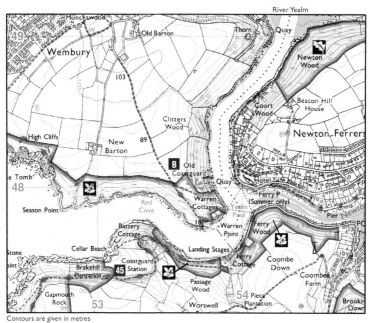

Contours are given in metres
The vertical interval is 10m

sprawling country house on a one-time gun position. On the seaward side, a path cuts down to Cellar Beach, a west-facing but usually sheltered cove. A row of coastguard cottages is passed. You now turn your back on houses – with one exception – for several miles, for this is the Revelstoke Drive **45**, a carefully engineered route round the cliffs which the Coast Path follows as far as Beacon Hill. Lord Revelstoke, whose home was at Membland, east of Noss Mayo, had this carriage drive cut in the 19th century by local fishermen. It encircled his property, and enabled him to impress his guests as he showed off his land. It makes an excellent high-level walking route.

The Coast Path enters Brakehill Plantation, and emerging at the west end, bears left and left again round first Mouthstone Point and then Gara Point. This is wonderful walking. The path is level and well surfaced, the views are magnificent, and in summer the gently sloping pasture between the path and the sea is a favoured habitat for birds, flowers and butterflies. These slopes are fenced off into large compartments for the better management of sheep flocks, and walkers must keep their dogs on leads. Cases of sheep being frightened over cliffs are not unknown.

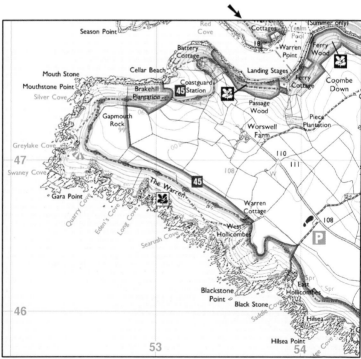

Contours are given in metres
The vertical interval is 10m

This stretch is known as the Warren, as in the 19th century it was managed for the propagation of rabbits. Warren Cottage, with its massive gateposts, is passed on the lower side. These distinctive gateposts are a feature of the South Hams, as this part of Devon, between Dartmoor and the English Channel, is known. Warren Cottage was built for the warrener who farmed the rabbits that bred on the cliffs.

Once round Blackstone Point a link path goes inland a few hundred yards to a National Trust car park, but the Coast Path continues eastwards, passing the disused Gunrow Signal Station. Buried nearby in the turf are the concrete bases of Second World War structures.

Just west of Stoke Point another link path heads north to a recently built car park, and then, having turned Stoke Point, the path leaves National Trust land and passes along a narrow vege-tated section, although the route of Revelstoke Drive **45** is still there beneath your feet.

A road and a car park are reached at Stoke House. The road leads down to the caravan site and the ruined and tucked-away church of St Peter the Poor Fisherman **46**. The diversion means a steep climb back again, but a visit to the partly restored church is well worth the effort.

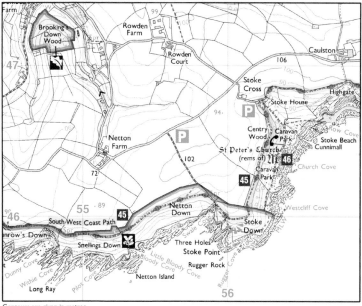

Contours are given in metres
The vertical interval is 10m

Now continue eastwards on the drive, here a terrace on the hillside, and in places rather poached by cattle. A view back reveals the caravan site and the church for those who did not go down the hill. The view ahead now includes Burgh Island, which is visited in the next chapter.

Where the Revelstoke Drive **45** turns inland at Beacon Hill a ruined folly built of stone with brick detailing is passed. This prominent feature is shown as Membland Pleasure House on Donn's map of 1765. The Coast Path here asserts itself once more and, 'freed from the shackles' of the Revelstoke Drive, plunges down to join a track visible ahead. This is possibly the steepest haul on the whole of the path, and is as unpleasant in descending as in ascending.

Where the farm track turns inland the Coast Path carries straight on, and is well waymarked through a succession of fields. St Anchorite's Rock beckons as a prominent feature on the coastline. However, a descent has to be negotiated first to the sheltered valley below Carswell, a verdant glen with its own little crag, Saddle Rock. St Anchorite's Rock is then reached, but disappoints on close acquaintance. It looks more impressive from a distance.

Heading eastwards, the Coast Path follows the hedge to a double stile. The next field is crossed, then the path bears right,

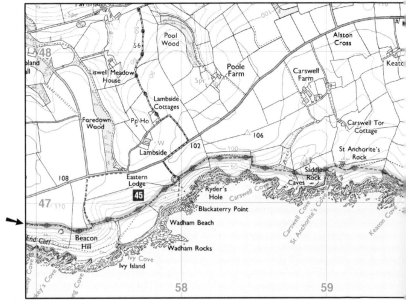

Contours are given in
The vertical interval

towards the cliff, and follows the edge down to Butcher's Cove where a cutting through the rock tells of farmers' forays to get sand and seaweed for the land. The path descends to sea level at Bugle Hole, then climbs steeply from the back of the cove up a zigzag.

The path now traces the field edge, keeping left of the fence, enters woods, then drops down towards Meadowsfoot (or Mothecombe) Beach. This beach is open to the public only on Wednesdays, Saturdays and Sundays, but walkers may follow the path to the far side of the beach where it strikes up through the woods of Owen's Hill, and down the other side to meet the road to the slipway and the ford across the mouth of the Erme.

Mothecombe is the hamlet near the car park, and is part of the Flete Estate through whose benign ownership the whole of this beautiful estuary has retained its tranquil atmosphere. The few houses, and the old coastguard cottages near the slipway, are the only dwellings, and no new buildings have been erected in the last century. The old school is open for refreshments in the summer. The two slipways and the Coast Path apart, there is no public access to the estuary.

In order to cross to Wonwell on the east bank there is only one way – it has to be waded. The alternative is a 9-mile (14.4-km) diversion inland round Sequers Bridge (see page 159).

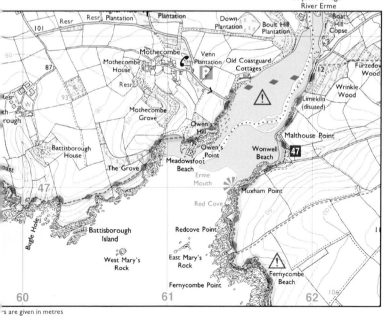

A CIRCULAR WALK ROUND THE REVELSTOKE DRIVE AT THE MOUTH OF THE YEALM

4¹/₄ miles (6.8 km)

From the National Trust's Warren Cliffs car park, pass out of the entrance, turn left and then right after 35 yards (32 metres) down an unmade road. This leads to Noss Mayo, an attractive village facing the larger settlement of Newton Ferrers across the tidal creek. Turn left opposite Noss Mayo car park, then right along a narrow road. After the last cottage on the left ascend the steps on the left, near a National Trust sign, into Fordhill Plantation. This path takes the walker off a narrow road, and should be followed to its end. Where the path rejoins the road (grid ref. 540476) – here the Revelstoke Drive **45** – turn right, and left after 25 yards (23 metres), to the ferry slip. Continue along a narrow path, through oak woods to a wide drive. Once through the gate the drive passes Battery Cottage, a country house, then enters Brakehill Plantation. When out of the trees, bear left around Mouthstone Point, then left again around Gara Point. Walk along the Warren, past Warren Cottage to Blackstone Point. Once past Blackstone Point, follow the link path inland back to the car park.

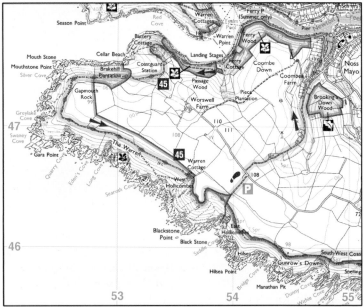

Scale approx 1 inch to ¹/₂ mile

Contours are given in metres
The vertical interval is 10m

Noss Mayo in the foreground, with Newton Ferrers in the background, at high tide.

Wembury Voluntary Marine Conservation Area

Wembury Point is about halfway along the Wembury Voluntary Marine Conservation Area, which stretches from Fort Bovisand to Gara Point, the headland to the east of the Great Mew Stone. Visitors are asked not to interfere with the marine life, which is rich in the shallow waters off the coast from Bovisand Bay to the mouth of the Yealm and was so threatened by recreational and educational activities that the whole area was designated a Voluntary Marine Conservation Area. Leaflets explaining the designation can be obtained from the Wembury Marine Centre behind Wembury Beach, which is managed by the Devon Wildlife Trust.

7 Wonwell to Salcombe

across the Avon Estuary
18¹/₂ miles (29.8 km)

The east side of the Erme Estuary is even less populated than the west side and the narrow approach lane to the slipway gives few opportunities for parking. Drivers must not obstruct the highway. The only pedestrian way across to the west side is to wade at low tide (see page 159).

Near the top of the east bank slipway a sign reads 'Coast Path Crossing Point 230m at Low Tide', and an arrow points out the direction. Opposite this notice a footpath sign indicates the Coast Path, and up a few steps the route goes into Wrinkle Wood and south along the side of the estuary. Leaving the wood, the fenced path continues to Wonwell Beach, where the ruins include a one-time pilot house **47**. Before the estuary silted up, small coasting vessels crept upriver with cargoes of limestone and coal for the lime kilns, and they needed a pilot to guide them past the constantly changing sand banks; the pilot lived in this cottage. You will notice that some embryo sand dunes are trying to establish themselves here. Up the side valley you can see the clogged ditches of water meadows when the light is right. Water was channelled along these carefully cut, gently descending leats, and when extra irrigation was required to provide an early bite, the banks were broken down and the water allowed to flow across the hillside. The indistinct lines of such ditches can be seen in many places in Devon, pointing to an agricultural practice now absent from the country calendar.

Muxham Point gives a superb view up the Erme, and there are some small rocky outcrops that provide good shelter for a picnic. The path is now clear all the way to Bigbury-on-Sea, and lies mostly between the cliff edge and the field fence. It is, however, a very strenuous stretch of the route, with severe undulations between Freshwater and Challaborough. Signs pointing in both directions warn of holes in the Coast Path caused by animals.

The first cove you meet is Westcombe Beach **A** and here a sign provided by the South Devon Coast and Countryside Service points to a route up the valley to Kingston. The building that you see here was a stable block for the horses when the Mildmay family, which has owned all the land fringing the Erme Estuary for over a century, came for picnics.

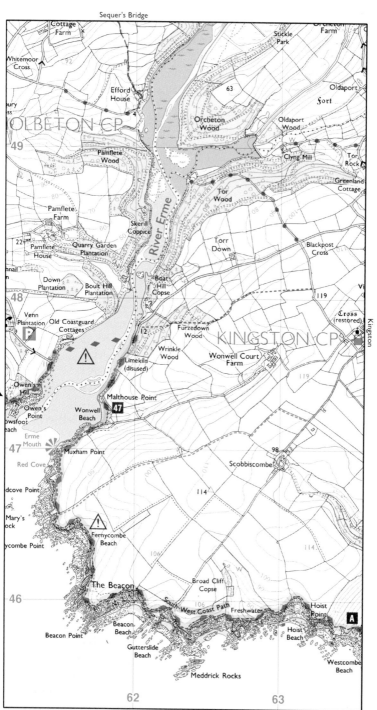

Sequer's Bridge

Cottage Farm

Whitemoor Cross

Efford House

Stickle Park

Orcheton Farm

63

Oldaport Fort

OLBETON CP

49

Orcheton Wood

Oldaport Wood

Pamflete Wood

Clyng Mill

Tor Rock

River Erme

Tor Wood

Greenland Cottage

Pamflete Farm

Skerill Coppice

Torr Down

224

Pamflete House

Quarry Garden Plantation

Blackpost Cross

hnail n

Down Plantation

Boult Hill Plantation

Boat Hill Copse

119

Vi

48

Venn Plantation

Old Coastguard Cottages

P

Furzedown Wood

Cross (restored)

Kingston

KINGSTON CP

12

Owen's Hill

Wrinkle Wood

Wonwell Court Farm

119

Owen's Point

Limekiln (disused)

Malthouse Point

owsfoot each

Wonwell Beach

47

Erme Mouth

47

Muxham Point

98

Red Cove

Scobbiscombe

dcove Point

114

Mary's ock

ycombe Point

Fernycombe Beach

114

106

The Beacon

Broad Cliff Copse

46

South West Coast Path

Freshwater

Hoist Point

Beacon Beach

Hoist Beach

A

Beacon Point

Gutterslide Beach

Westcombe Beach

Meddrick Rocks

62

63

Contours are given in metres
The vertical interval is 10m

BIGBURY BAY

95

After a climb, descend to Ayrmer Cove where two paths head inland to Ringmore. This is the village where R.C. Sherriff wrote *Journey's End*, his play about the First World War, and the pub is named after it. Over the next hill and down the other side is the expansive family holiday village of Challaborough – by a topographical trick not noticed from the west until one is almost there. The Coast Path goes round the back of the beach and on to Bigbury-on-Sea; another popular holiday resort with masses of sand. Youth hostellers are warned that the hostel which used to operate here was closed a few years ago.

If time allows, the walker should stroll across the sands to Burgh Island **48**. Even if the tide is in, the island may still be reached for a few pence by using the sea tractor.

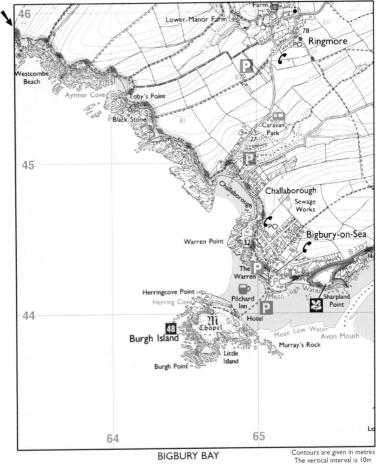

BIGBURY BAY

Contours are given in metres
The vertical interval is 10m

From Bigbury, if you are heading east, you need to cross the mouth of the Avon to reach Bantham **49** (see page 159), and if the tide is low you may walk along the sands beneath the cliffs. However, if the tide is high, or coming in, there is a risk of being cut off, and you should walk up the road – diverting briefly around the pleasant 7 acres (2.8 hectares) of the National Trust's Clematon Hill property – and go up the road to Folly Farm. Turn in where you see a sign giving the ferry times, and follow the Coast Path down to Cockleridge, an open dune-like area. The ferry crosses to Bantham from the southern tip of Cockleridge.

Having crossed, there is an opportunity to look at Bantham **49**, once something of a port, but now given over to beach fun. The area is owned by the Evans Estates. The quay at Bantham is now used only by small-boat sailors.

From the road above the ferry (south side) the Coast Path loops around the sandspit (the Ham), although you could cut this off and go straight on through the car park and out to the headland at the south end of Bantham Sands. Bathing can be dangerous here. Having rounded the point beyond the lifeguards' hut, the path climbs to the ridge whose western end is the Long

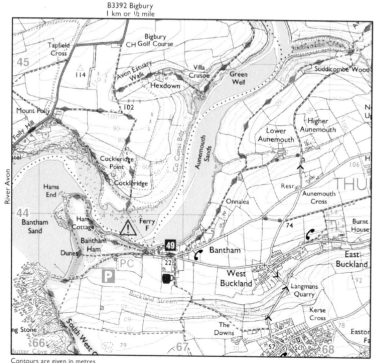

Contours are given in metres
The vertical interval is 10m

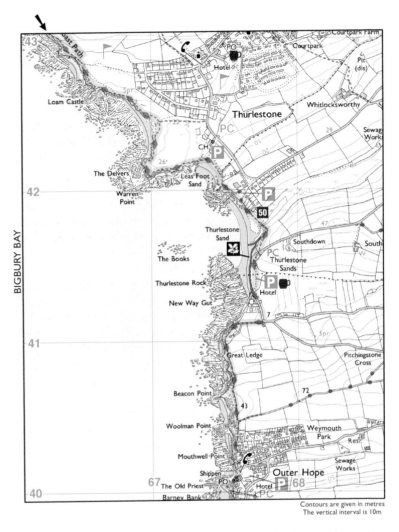

Contours are given in metres
The vertical interval is 10m

Stone, a prominent seashore stack. Bolt Tail beckons a few miles ahead, and Malborough Church spire reminds you that Salcombe is about 2 miles (3.2 km) beyond its ancient pinnacle.

Soon you have the golf course for company. This section has a rich variety of plants and insects. Large areas of wild white clover, sea thrift, marguerite daisies and many other species attract a profusion of butterflies.

Along here there is a string of sandy bays, not all of which are named on maps. They are, from north to south, Broad Sand, Yarner Sand, Leasfoot Sand, and Thurlestone Sand (also called South Milton Sands). Leasfoot Sand is backed by a large car park and the clubhouse of the golf course. The wreck lying off it is that of the *Louis Sheid*, a famous name in South Devon lifeboat history after it went aground in December 1939, having saved 62 survivors from the Dutch passenger ship *Tajandoen*.

The Coast Path goes seaward of a large block of flats, Links Court (once the Links Hotel), passes a car park, and drops to cross South Milton Ley by an 80-yard (73-metre) footbridge. South Milton Ley **50** is the second largest reed bed in Devon, and is managed by the Devon Bird Watching and Preservation Society. The footbridge is a good place from which to observe reed and sedge warblers, moorhens and herons.

From South Milton Sands car park the Coast Path has to go slightly inland, past a new apartment complex, and then it returns to the coast beside a hotel. The way is now clear due south to Outer Hope, which is coupled to its twin, Inner Hope, by a link path below the Cottage Hotel.

The Coast Path goes up from the lifeboat house at Inner Hope and out through National Trust land to Bolt Tail, which, to prevent damage to the Iron Age earthwork, should be entered by the original entrance about halfway along the embankment. Proceed to the tip of Bolt Tail. Now turn and head east, past Redrot Cove and Ramillies **51**, named after the naval ship which drove into the cliffs. Then go up the fenced-off cliff path towards Graystone with its views back to the north-west.

The path rises to Bolberry Down, where there is a large National Trust car park (the whole of the coastline from Bolt Tail to Bolt Head is owned by the National Trust).

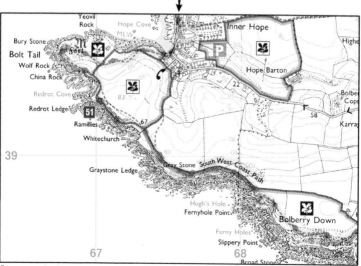

Contours are given in metres
The vertical interval is 10m

Soar Mill Cove, looking west towards Bolberry Down.

From the east end of the Bolberry Down car park the Coast Path continues along the crest of a rocky spine, with the cliffs on one side and a sheep-grazed valley on the other. The outcrop of Hazel Tor is across the valley. One is very conscious of the rock here – it is mica schist, of a type that fractures into flat or longitudinal pieces. Slabs used to be raised on edge and made into primitive field boundaries and you can see some along here.

The Coast Path now drops down to the back of Soar Mill Cove **52**, and at the foot of the descent note the large timber gatepost. It bears an incised inscription reading 'Certified to accommodate 4 seamen' and was washed ashore in the cove some years ago. Out to sea you will notice the Ham Stone **53**, which the four-masted barque the *Herzogin Cecilie* struck in April 1936.

The beach here is attractive to bathers at certain states of the tide, but swimmers should not go out too far. The setting of the cove in a totally unspoilt situation makes it a desirable destination for those who scorn items such as deckchairs, fun floats and refreshment kiosks. Instead, its devotees make do with natural attractions, such as the spring squill that blooms here.

A climb out of the valley eastwards, keeping close to the cliffs, brings the walker up to the Warren. Follow the well-trodden route along the top of the cliffs, rather than the public footpath running parallel but a little inland. The views are much better, and one sees rocky outcrops, such as the Goat, which punctuate the sidelands between Steeple Cove and Off Cove.

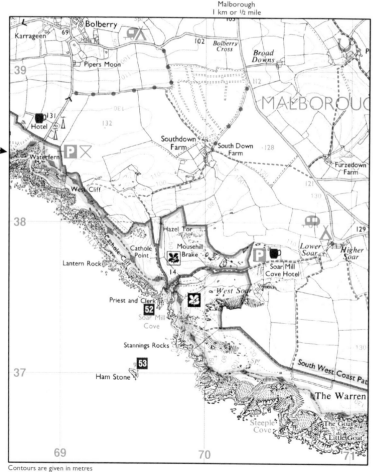

Contours are given in metres
The vertical interval is 10m

This high-level path now meets the more inland route. Cross over a stile, then a path across a small field takes you to another stile (the lower of the two), which leads to yet another stile, on the other side of which the path heads down a grassy gulley towards the knobbly point of Bolt Head. A Second World War lookout and accommodation block are built into the rocks.

From the foot of the ravine the Coast Path bears round to the north, and for the first time you can see the next stretch of coastline to be walked, from East Portlemouth to Prawle Point.

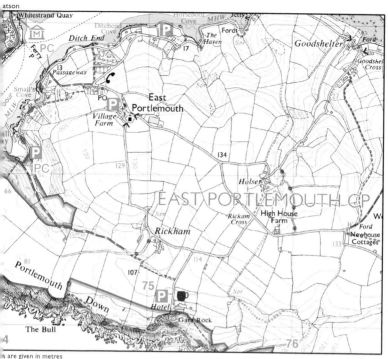

The path descends to the back of Starehole Bay, then turns 90 degrees eastwards to pass round the spiky crags of Sharp Tor. This is the Courtenay Walk, a path cut by a member of the Courtenay family in the 19th century to give access to Bolt Head.

A straightforward walk of 2 miles (3.2 km) now brings the walker into Salcombe (see page 105), a haven for anyone interested in small boats. The Coast Path soon passes the entrance to Overbecks **B**. This early-20th-century house and 6 acres (2.4 hectares) of beautiful garden were left to the National Trust in 1937 by Mr Otto Overbeck. Much of the house is used as Salcombe Youth Hostel, and in the rest is a small museum of local bygones. The mild climate enables unusual plants to be grown. Overbecks' garden is designated a Grade II garden in the English Heritage *Register of Parks and Gardens of Special Historic Interest*.

The rest of the route into Salcombe is along narrow roads which are frequently busy. In season a ferry runs from South Sands to the town quay, from where you can walk back through the centre of the town to the ferry across to East Portlemouth. For details of the ferry services at Salcombe to East Portlemouth, see page 159.

A CIRCULAR WALK AROUND BOLT HEAD

4 miles (6.4 km)

From the car park at the National Trust property of Overbecks **B** at the south end of Salcombe, walk down the hill, the way you drove up, turning sharp right at the bottom. Follow the Courtenay Walk out to Sharp Tor and on to Bolt Head. From the tip of Bolt Head, walk north-west up the grassy ravine and follow the Coast Path around to the left and over a stile. The path bears right, round Off Cove, crosses another stile to enter a field, then leaves it at its south-west corner. Now follow the wall right – the Coast Path diverges away to the left – and after 500 yards (460 metres) turn right, off the open land, along a path going past the derelict buildings of Middle Soar to a road. Turn left here, then right, along a straight track beyond a gravel depot. At the end of the track turn right, then left over a stile signposted YHA and to Salcombe. This is a National Trust permissive path. Follow the path straight across several fields and stiles, then left at a path signposted to Overbecks. Walk north between a fence and hedge to a stile, where you turn right, and go down to Overbecks car park and back to the start of the walk.

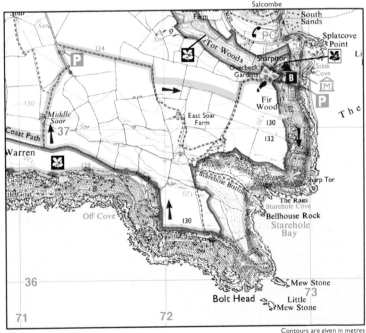

Contours are given in metres
The vertical interval is 10m

Salcombe

The visitor could be excused for thinking that Salcombe has a history stretching back to ancient times, but this would be wrong. Until the early 19th century it was East Portlemouth on the opposite shore that was the dominant settlement, and Batson, at the head of the first creek to the north of Salcombe, also has pretensions to a past. Salcombe became established as a shipbuilding town for the racy fruit schooners that were built along the waterfront. These speedy craft had to be capable of quick trips to bring the fruit to England in good condition from the Azores, West Indies and the Mediterranean. At the same time, early holidaymakers were coming to Devon's southern-most town for its mild climate. There is a castle here, it is true; another of those built by Henry VIII to defend the harbour and anchorage. It had to wait for action until 1643, when it came into its own during the Civil War.

Visitors now come to Salcombe in great numbers, by sea as well as by land, and the many-tentacled Kingsbridge Estuary, or Salcombe Harbour, as the different components are called, provides sheltered moorings and scope for much natural-history interest. The estuary is in fact a ria, or drowned valley. No large rivers find their way into its waters, so the salinity is undiluted. At the head of the tidal waters is Kingsbridge, a busy market town, and the focus for life in this part of Devon.

Salcombe waterfront.

8 East Portlemouth to Torcross

past Prawle Point and Hallsands
13 1/2 miles (21.7 km)

From the ferry landing at East Portlemouth walk up to the minor road and turn right (south). In one-third of a mile (500 metres) this brings you to Mill Bay where there is a fine stretch of sand at low tide. In fact, when the tide is out there is a string of sandy coves stretching for about a mile along the east shore of Salcombe Harbour. At high tide they disappear, except for Mill Bay.

The Coast Path leaves Mill Bay by the lower path option through the woods. The higher path runs parallel and the two meet up 1 1/2 miles (2.4 km) further on, but the lower path gives closer contact with the sea. Much of the route between here and Prawle Point is on National Trust land.

The path now heads east with the agricultural land of Portlemouth Down stretching inland from the higher path. Until the late 19th century this area was divided into hundreds of small

Disused thatched lookout, Gara Rock Hotel.

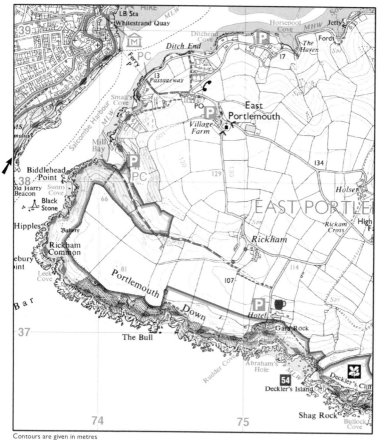

Contours are given in metres
The vertical interval is 10m

strip fields, but these were swept away and some time later a golf course was established there, which has now also gone.

This length of path is a good place to observe the dodder, a parasitic plant displaying tiny flowers and a mass of red capillary tendrils, which seems to be suffocating its host plant, the gorse, like an all-enveloping hairnet. Kestrels and ravens are likely to be seen overhead, and shags and cormorants congregate on a shoreline rock.

Below the Gara Rock Hotel – once coastguard cottages, and still boasting a preserved thatched lookout – the lower path keeps the walker nearest the sea, and drops to Rickham Sands **54**, a pleasant place for a bathe. Decklers Cliff to the east has recently been found by the National Trust's archaeologists to have a previously unsuspected field system, possibly medieval or earlier.

Beyond Decklers Cliff a path descends to Moor Sands, an even more isolated cove than Rickham Sands. Offshore from here a 'historic wreck' has been designated **55**, which is believed to date from Bronze Age times, say 3,000 years ago at least.

For some obscure reason, a succession of place names having a porcine theme is passed – Pig's Nose, Ham Stone (another!) and Gammon Head. The name Pig's Nose is also preserved in the name of a pub in East Prawle, the inside of which is decorated with dozens of postcards depicting pigs. Gammon Head is the most distinctive headland on the south coast of Devon, a rocky spur sheltering Maceley Cove, the apotheosis of the remote sandy cove. This delectable beach can only be reached by a scramble, but the experience will not disappoint.

The Coast Path continues around the back of Elender Cove and climbs steeply abreast of Signalhouse Point to reach Devon's southernmost headland, Prawle Point **56**, by the coastguard lookout. Signalhouse Point was bought by the National Trust in 1985. The purpose of the 'Signal House' is unknown, but the ruins of a small structure can be seen on the clifftop, and the first edition 1-inch Ordnance Survey map shows a building with a track leading to it.

The map in this guide shows a number of long narrow fields between the coast and Prawle Point lane, 'behind' Signalhouse

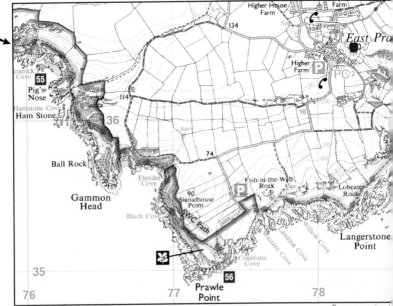

Contours are given i
The vertical interval

Point. Unfortunately these walls were bulldozed over the cliff before coming into the Trust's ownership. The orthostat walls, made of flat upright stones set on edge, which continued these field boundaries down the sidelands, still remain.

Prawle Point means 'lookout hill', and it has been a vantage point against invaders since early times. Nowadays the National Coastwatch Institution operates the watch house here. There is a small separate building offering shelter and information and it is possible to buy bottled water from the officer on duty.

East from here for several miles the Coast Path follows a low, level route. A succession of fields is entered, tracing the path which is always on the seaward side of the crops. For nearly 2 miles (3.2 km), the Torrs, the early Pleistocene cliff line, rear up to your left (north). Once past the isolated Maelcombe House, the path carries on around Woodcombe Point, and the pinnacle

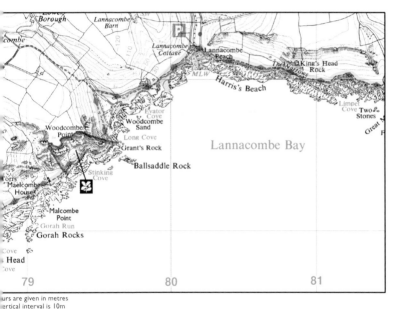

urs are given in metres
ertical interval is 10m

on its west side is worth looking out for. In the Woodcombe Valley a path heads inland, but the Coast Path, after doglegging north, continues eastwards, passing behind one house then in front of what may have been coastguard cottages with a lookout.

Lannacombe is a popular beach in summer, and cars penetrate down the valley although space is limited. A water mill and lime kiln operated here at one time. The next stretch is due east along the Narrows to Great Mattiscombe Sand (pronounced Matchcombe), and the landmarks to look out for just west of the beach are the Pinnacles, isolated stacks of glacial head on schist bases. This is an attractive beach, although dangerous for swimming; cars cannot reach it, but there is a car park at Start Farm one-third of a mile (500 metres) north.

The Coast Path now negotiates the headland and goes on to Start Point, an exhilarating walk between frost-sculpted rock-faces on one side and disturbed sea on the other. This is a wild scene, where one feels very close to elemental forces.

Round the corner, Start Point Lighthouse **57** comes into view, a reminder of the hazards of the coast. It stands, soap-powder white, at the end of a cock's-comb ridge of schist. The name Start in this case comes from the Anglo-Saxon word *steort* meaning a tail, an element found in the name of the bird, the redstart. The lighthouse was built in 1836.

Once again, a different view now presents itself. The gently parabolic sweep of Start Bay is lined up roughly south to north, giving a very direct route onwards. Go up the light-house road to the car park at Start Farm, and cross the stile opposite. There now follows a good uncomplicated path as far as Hallsands, with an encouraging vista pulling the walker forward.

Hallsands is two places: the 'new' settlement on the clifftop; and the old ruined village on the rock ledge below **58** (see page 113). The remains of the old road take you down to a viewing platform where the tragic history of Hallsands is told.

The Coast Path passes in front of Trouts and goes behind the Hallsands Hotel, coming out at Greenstraight, the first of three shingle beaches, each larger than the last, which the walker has to follow.

The Coast Path continues north over Tinsey Head, an easy walk, and Beesands **59** is reached, passing between cottages at the south end of the village. This linear settlement is now protected by massive boulders and a newly erected sea defence wall, for in the recent past it has suffered, like the villages on either side, from the occasional furious easterly gales.

The path continues past the small lake known as Widdicombe Ley. The name defines its use as a provider of withies since Domesday. From Beesands Cellars, at the north end of the beach

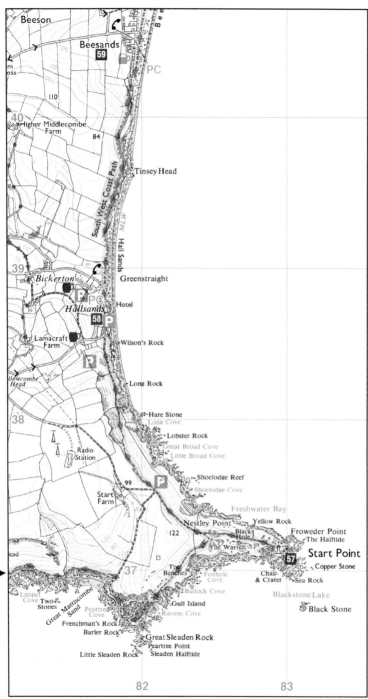

Contours are given in metres
The vertical interval is 10m

111

and an indication of fish curing in the past, the path goes up behind the house called Sunnydale on the map. (There was also a lime kiln here at one time.) It then climbs up around the back of an old quarry. This is owned by the National Trust, and can be entered from the beach if there is time in the walking schedule. Another possibility, if the tide is low, is to walk along the pebbles to Torcross, but this can be more tiring than slogging up and around the quarry!

Assuming the true Coast Path has been followed, the route zigzags down to Torcross through a tangle of house drives and steps, and there is a choice over the last hundred yards or so. The path comes down – and this should be noted by the east-to-west walker – either by the steps at the south end of the sea wall, or by the public toilets.

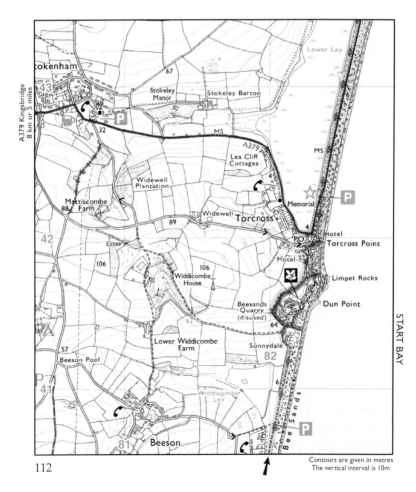

Contours are given in metres
The vertical interval is 10m

Torcross, with Slapton Ley behind and Slapton Sands in front.

Hallsands

For perhaps three or four hundred years until early last century the houses of Hallsands **58** stood in a row above the beach, secure on their rocky ledge and protected by a shingle foreshore. However, in 1897 the contractor responsible for construction work at Devonport Dockyard was given permission to dredge shingle offshore, from the Skerries Bank. In a very short time 500,000 tons were taken, and the beach level dropped 12 feet (3.7 metres) before dredging stopped in 1902. Its natural defences dissipated, the village was exposed to the sea, and over several years all but two of the 37 houses were wrecked.

Torcross

Torcross is an important place astride the Coast Path. The A379 is met here, there are buses, large car parks, shops, a post office, pubs, restaurants and accommodation. The village is really inseparable from Slapton Ley **60** (see page 127), the stretch of water beside it, but it has been more concerned, historically, with the sea, which nearly demolished the village in 1951 and 1979. The present massive concrete wall dates from 1980.

9 Torcross to Brixham

through Dartmouth and Kingswear
21¹/₂ miles (34.6 km)

Beyond Torcross – assuming you are progressing from west to east – the character of the Coast Path changes. For 2¹/₂ miles (4 km) the route runs alongside the A379, which is not as bad as it sounds, as the path is off the road.

You are following Slapton Sands, or the Line as it is known locally, which is really shingle, and on the inland side is Slapton Ley **60** (see page 127), although there is nothing to prevent you from following the seaward side if you wish.

After about 1¹/₂ miles (2.4 km) a road turns west to the village of Slapton. The parish was recorded at the time of Domesday (1086) and continues to thrive 900 years later. In the village, the dominant building is the 80-foot (24-metre) tower of Sir Guy de Brien's chantry, which he founded in 1372. This was served by four priests whose duty was to ensure that the mass was said for Sir Guy's soul in perpetuity. There is much good building in the village, which has a shop, a post office and two inns. The causeway linking the village to the Sands is of fairly recent construction. On the Sands, where the causeway now joins them, there used to be Slapton Cellars, a base for the local fishermen, and a lime kiln. The cellars became the Royal Sands Hotel, but were severely damaged in 1940 when a dog set off some land mines. Invasion practice later in the war completed its demolition.

Just beyond the T-junction a stone memorial **61** marks the use of seven parishes in the Slapton hinterland for invasion practice by the US forces in 1943. The Coast Path now crosses the A379 to the seaward side and follows the old route of the road. In 2001 a storm washed away parts of the road and it was decided to reroute the path on the Ley side. After a while you cross back again on to the original route.

Cross the road again at Strete Gate, where the road veers away from the coast. The Coast Path climbs from here, going to the right of the car park. The place name Strete Gate refers to the time when the Line was used for grazing, and a fence and gate were constructed at the north end of the Sands to control the animals. The site is now a picnic area, and panels provided by the South Devon Coast and Countryside Service give information about the history of this end of the sands.

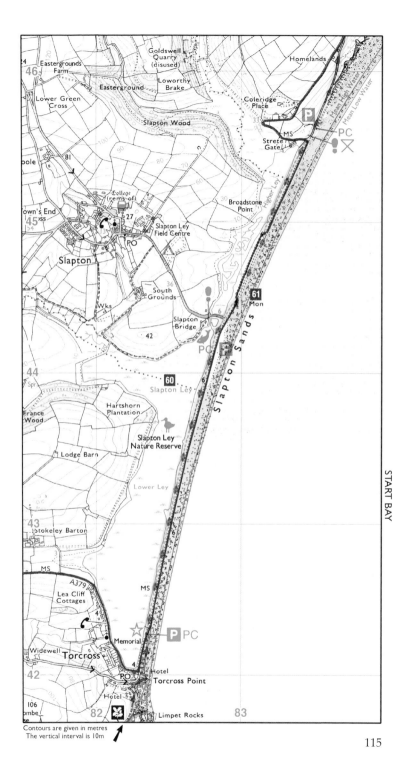

START BAY

Contours are given in metres
The vertical interval is 10m

115

Blackpool Sands.

At the north end of Slapton Sands, three-quarters of a mile (1.2 km) beyond Strete Gate, is the site of Undercliffe, another lost village, which probably met its end in 1703. However, from Strete Gate the path cuts a corner off the A379, but rejoins it one-third of a mile (500 metres) further on.

At the time of writing (2002) there are plans to reroute the Coast Path from here to the other side of Stoke Fleming, bringing it closer to the sea. Nothing has been finalised yet, but do look out for new signs at the north end of Slapton Sands, and at Warren Point.

Until then, the Coast Path still climbs to the A379 at the western end of Strete. This is a busy bit of road, especially in the summer, so walkers must stay in single file, face oncoming traffic, and keep their wits about them. At the first turning left (north), go up Hynetown Road, and follow it round to Strete Church.

Turn left here, then shortly turn right and keep on this way-marked bridleway for some distance while it leads north, then east, then south, before rejoining the A379.

Follow the road around a sharp turn to the right and then take the first turning left at a wall letter-box, back on to the waymarked route. Keep right at the next fork, down a lane that deteriorates to a track after Widewell. At the bottom turn sharp right (east) and a main road (the A379) is soon reached at Blackpool Sands.

From where the Coast Path meets the main road it is followed for about 100 yards (90 metres) or so, and the turning north taken by a thatched cottage. This quiet valley-bottom road is followed for a quarter of a mile (400 metres), then turn right (east) up a public bridleway opposite the bridge leading to Blackpool Farm. This is a steep rocky lane called Mill Lane, which leads in two-thirds of a mile (1 km) to Stoke Fleming Church.

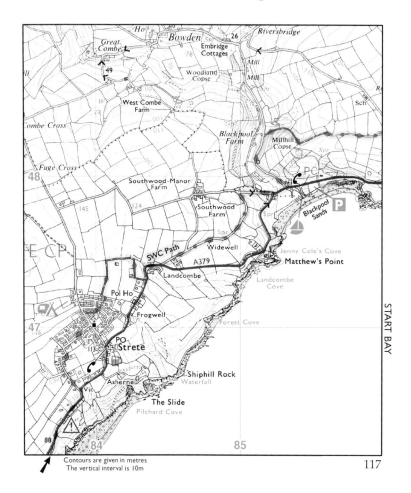

Contours are given in metres
The vertical interval is 10m

117

Opposite the church gate turn down Rectory Lane, and enter a footpath at the end by the rectory gate. This brings you to Venn Lane, where you turn right and almost immediately left along Ravensbourne Lane. At the bus shelter turn left and immediately right along a narrow minor road.

Little Dartmouth is reached at a National Trust car park on both sides of the road. Turn right (south) through the newer car park (which was once a tennis court) and follow the path to the coast through a number of gates. Having once more reached the cliffs a fine view unfolds: Start Point to the right, and across the mouth of the Dart to the cliffs east of Kingswear to the left.

The Coast Path now bears east then north, passes round the back of Compass Cove, and dips to sea level via a stile. The path contours round to Blackstone Point, crossing a sea-washed gulley by a footbridge, then climbs gently to meet the minor road at Compass Cottage, with fine views to the right across the River Dart.

At Compass Cottage, turn right, then right again, descending down a zigzag path almost to sea level at Sugary Cove. Now climb back up, reaching the road again by the entrance to the National Trust's Gallants Bower property. This is the wooded hill that is such a conspicuous feature in the view from Dartmouth itself. From the Gallants Bower car park, descend the steps to the lower road above Dartmouth Castle **62**, which can be visited. It was built in the 1480s to defend the town against attack from the sea. The Coast Path winds down between the buildings to the church and then follows the road round to Warfleet, where it descends to an old quay with lime kilns. Walk under the

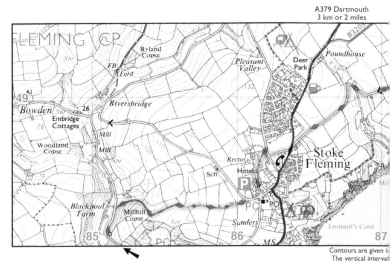

arch and up some steps to rejoin the road. The route into Dartmouth passes some fine buildings and offers pleasant views of Kingswear. At Bayard's Castle go down steps, walk through the castle remains and emerge on to a quay.

In order to cross Dartmouth Harbour refer to page 159. The lower vehicle ferry can be used, or a passenger ferry operates from just a short way upriver. Both ferries arrive in Kingswear near the railway station. Run as the Torbay and Dartmouth Steam Railway, in season trains run to Paignton on Great Western Railway principles. Maypool Youth Hostel is 3 miles (4.8 km) north of here.

DARTMOUTH

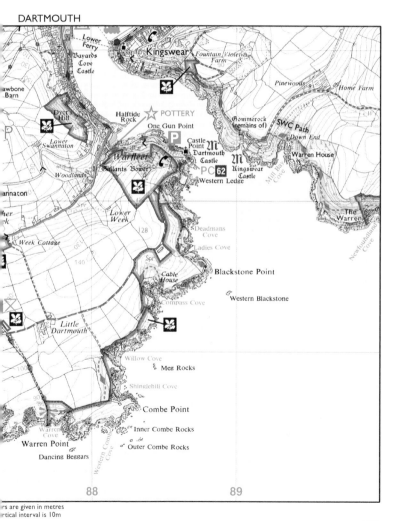

rs are given in metres
rtical interval is 10m

To continue along the Coast Path, pass under the arch by the ferry slip and go up Alma Steps, turning right (east) along Beacon Road. The road narrows to a path and gradually ascends to meet a road where you should continue east, past the small National Trust property of Inverdart.

After following what is normally a quiet road for half a mile (800 metres) the road turns inland, and 50 yards (45 metres) or so beyond the bend, take a flight of timber steps leading down into the valley. Beside the steps is a memorial plaque **63** to Lt-Col H. Jones, VC, OBE. After his death in the Falklands, it was agreed that a new length of Coast Path, from near Kingswear Castle to Newfoundland Cove, should be opened in his memory; he had strong family associations in the area. Thus it was that this splendid length of path was opened, beginning (or ending) at the ingenious timber steps built by Alan Pope. The memorial was unveiled by Jones's widow in July 1984.

For the next 6 miles (9.6 km), as far as Sharkham Point, the coast is one of the most beautiful stretches along the entire National Trail. Much of it is owned by the National Trust, and there should be no route-finding problems. Link paths head inland to convenient car parks, but it is a strenuous piece of walking.

At the foot of the first descent is Mill Bay, with a small castellated building (marked 'Dangerous'), which used to be a mill. The path climbs steeply up, and enters a Devon Wildlife Trust Nature Reserve.

After about 1¹/₂ miles (2.4 km) walking among the Monterey pines, the path levels out, with good views right across Start Bay, and enters National Trust property (the Higher Brownstone on the omega sign refers to a nearby farm) above Newfoundland Cove. Once round the back of the cove the walk ascends to a flat grassy plot with a signpost, surrounded on three sides by Second World War buildings. This was Inner Froward Point Coast Defence Battery **64**. Go to the seat in front of the lookout hut, the one with the steel drop-down shutters: this is a wonderful viewpoint. The island is the Mew Stone. Some buildings are still scattered around among the trees, and there were many more, probably Nissen huts, but all that remain are their concrete bases.

From here there is a choice of paths heading east. The quick, straightforward route is to leave the grassy plot at the east end, but instead of turning up the steep Military Road, carry on along the signposted path within the woods. After about 300 yards (275 metres) the lower, longer, and more interesting diversion rejoins this higher path from below. The directions for the lower path from the grassy plot are as follows: descend a wartime brick path to the west of the lookout hut, passing two shell magazines, two gun positions and a shell incline, until you almost reach sea level and two searchlight emplacements. The lower path proceeds eastwards, then zigzags up to rejoin the higher path.

Turn right (east) here, go over a stile and after a short distance, in a dip, turn right. The higher path leads to a viewpoint on a small eminence, behind Outer Froward Point, from which there is a view inland of the Tower, an 80-foot (24-metre) hollow stone daytime navigational aid built in 1864. The Coast Path contours round Outer Froward Point, giving good views of the Mew Stone, before crossing a small stream at the back of Old Mill Bay.

Just before Pudcombe Cove a link path from Coleton Farm joins the Coast Path, which now drops steeply into the Coleton Fishacre Valley **65** (see page 126) and up the other side. Access to Coleton Fishacre garden can be gained in the summer on Wednesdays, Fridays and Sundays between 11 a.m. and 6 p.m., and non-Trust members should pay at the main entrance. Coleton Fishacre House was built in 1925–6 by Rupert D'Oyly Carte, son of the Gilbert and Sullivan impresario.

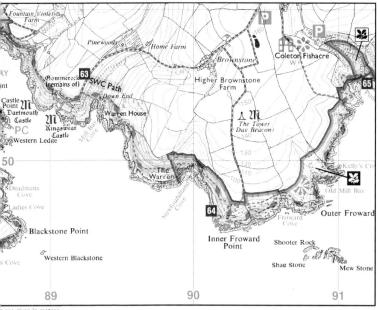

Because the Coast Path runs across the grain of the land there is much up and down walking, but a number of link paths make opting out a possibility without trespassing on crops. Between Newfoundland Cove and Sharkham Point there are two small stretches of coast that are not owned by the Trust; they lie between Scabbacombe Head and Scabbacombe Sands, and to the east of Southdown Cliff. Man Sands Cottages are also privately owned.

You leave the wooded area by a squeeze stile and continue a switchback course along the cliffs, aided by waymarks. Above the deep indentation of Ivy Cove another link path heads inland to a car park at Coleton Camp **66**, also a wartime site. The next valley is remarkable for the number of hedges that were removed some years ago, to be replaced by fences, so the area looks like an escaped piece of Dorset downland.

At the next fork in the path take the lower route, unless you are following the National Trust permissive path back to Coleton Camp. This link path follows a line of hedgerows westwards from Scabbacombe Head.

A steep drop down to Scabbacombe Sands – a delightful cove for a bathe – is followed by another uphill climb above Long Sands. (Yet another link path goes inland to a National Trust car park in Scabbacombe Lane.) After this a fine free-wheeling stretch brings you down to Man Sands. Two rough approaches (four if you count the Coast Path), its proximity to Brixham and a row of coastguard cottages converted to holiday use make this beach more popular than Scabbacombe Sands. Both are of shingle, and neither has any 'facilities'. There is an old lime kiln at Man Sands. The beach back was repaired with gabions by the National Trust in 1987.

The climb up Southdown Cliff is steep, but soon levels out and then descends by a new piece of path that weaves its way down what was once a steep incline. After passing through a stile the way is clear to Sharkham Point.

Sharkham Point has survived because it is mostly made of hard rocks. This much-visited headland is a geological curiosity: a complex of rock types in a small area. St Mary's Bay, once called Mudstone Bay, backs up against slatey material, which is less resistant. As one looks north from Sharkham Point the change in scenery is very evident. The South Devon holiday area is near at hand, and from here onwards, with a break between Torquay and Shaldon, the trappings of tourism are never far away.

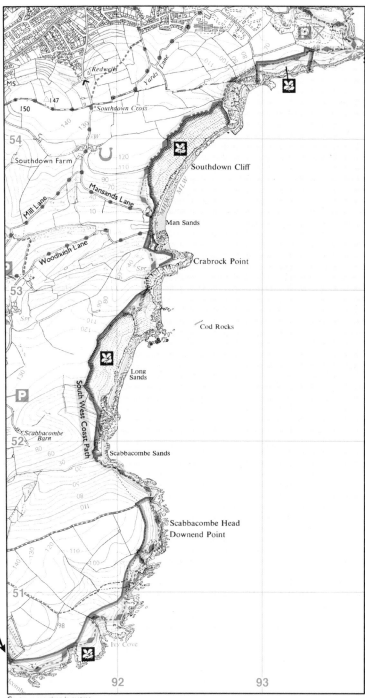

Contours are given in metres
The vertical interval is 10m

123

From the northern base of Sharkham Point the Coast Path goes down a once-tarmaced road, then up to the left to follow the back of the bay round on a variety of surfaces. Keeping the holiday parks on the left, the next landmark is Durl Head, offering views of another Mew Stone.

Berry Head is getting nearer, and the approach across the common and in through the main gate is recommended. The whole area is now a country park and there is a great deal to see. It is difficult to know where to start, and on a fine day the walker should be prepared to spend an hour or two looking around – at the view, and at the objects of interest near at hand.

The cliffs give good nesting sites for sea birds. Kittiwakes are the noisiest; fulmars have the most attractive flight; guillemots, razorbills, shags and various kinds of gull are also present, so binoculars are useful.

The name Berry is a corruption of the Saxon word *Byri* or *Byrig*, meaning castle or fortification, and until the Napoleonic War fort was built, an Iron Age earthwork and ditch could be seen across the neck of the headland. (Even earlier remains were found in a cave on the approach from Brixham. This is not open to the public.) Unfortunately, when the fort was built the engineer in charge scraped the western approach clean to give a good field of fire, so it is unlikely that much remains to be discovered.

An orientation table at the tip of Berry Head states that Portland Bill is 42 miles (67.5 km) away. Near this useful device is Berry Head Lighthouse, the shortest in the Trinity House service but, after all, it is 190 feet (58 metres) above sea level. Worth seeking out behind the coastguard lookout is the old sentry box, in as good repair now as when it was built. Over the wall from the sentry box is the disused Berry Head limestone quarry. Work ceased here in 1969.

Refreshments are served in the old guardroom from Easter to the end of October. Inland, an aircraft navigation beacon gives a science-fiction feel to the area.

When you have been to the end and seen everything, return to the main gate and, having passed through, turn right (northwest) along a tarmac track, but where the track passes into the disused quarry, carry on down a gravel path, bearing left and staying on the main path through the woodland.

The road is reached by a circular enclosure now used as a car park. This was a wartime fuel storage tank that had its roof removed. The large hotel was built as the hospital for the Berry Head fort garrison, and was later lived in by the Rev. Henry Francis Lyte of 'Abide With Me' fame.

Stay on the road until you reach a car park. Go through the car park and down to a walkway beside some gardens, past the outdoor swimming pool. The road is rejoined for a short stretch before steps take you down to a waterfront walkway heading into the town centre.

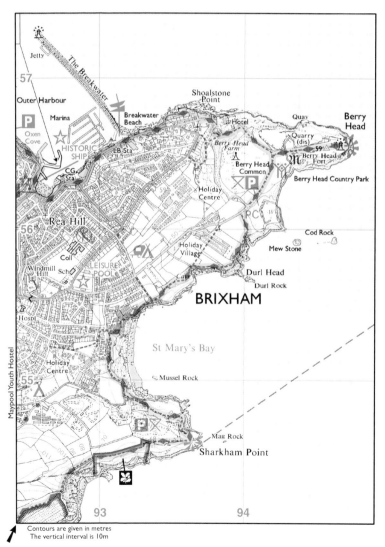

Contours are given in metres
The vertical interval is 10m

A CIRCULAR WALK ROUND THE COAST AT COLETON FISHACRE

3¾ miles (6.1 km)

From the National Trust car park near Higher Brownstone Farm, walk south along the Military Road, past the Tower (see page 121) to the Inner Froward Point Coast Defence Battery **64**. Now walk east along the Coast Path observing the various high or low path options (see page 121), crossing Coleton Fishacre Valley **65**, and going on to use the link path inland from the back of Ivy Cove (which is signposted). Coleton wartime camp **66** is reached – it is now a car park – and the farm track followed to the road at the Coleton Fishacre crossroads. Carry on across the junction and the car park is reached in a quarter of a mile (400 metres).

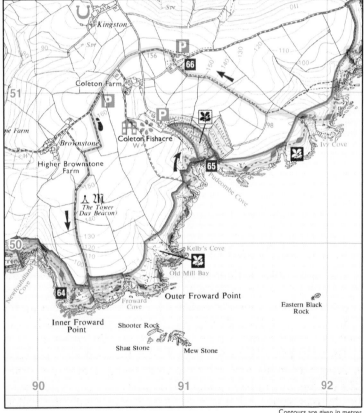

Contours are given in metres
The vertical interval is 10m

Water lilies and swans at the nature reserve of Slapton Ley, Devon's largest natural freshwater lake.

Slapton Sands and Ley

The shingle banks of Slapton Sands, Beesands and Greenstraight, and of Chesil Beach in Dorset, originated just after the last Ice Age, when the glaciers melted. Sea levels rose and swept up the material to form the barrier beaches of the present coast. Prior to that the rising land behind the Ley **60** was the coastline.

The line of small concrete posts beside the road was erected to prevent the fragile turf and flora from being damaged by cars. The succession of plants going inland from the sea-washed shingle is interesting and much studied. Starting with the yellow horned poppy, which binds the loose material with its long roots, the progression continues with sand couch grass, sea beet, rest harrow, Danish scurvy grass and rock samphire. Several small fenced areas are set aside to observe the effect when human and animal access is denied.

It is difficult to separate the Sands (the cause) from the Ley (the effect). Slapton Ley is the most extensive natural freshwater lake in Devon, and is a National Nature Reserve; it became a protected area for birds as long ago as 1896. The Field Studies Council established a Field Centre between the Ley and the village, and this is the base for using the reserve as a conservation, educational, research and recreational resource. Many hundreds of students of all ages attend Slapton Ley Field Centre as residents each year, but there are also displays and facilities for the casual visitor, and trails to walk.

The Ley is not more than 9 feet (2.7 metres) deep and is heavily silted. Eels and pike grow to a large size, and the pike keep the frogs and ducklings in check. Great crested grebe and Cetti's warbler are two of the birds that have recently started to breed here, but the list of resident and migrant species is lengthy.

A cause for concern in recent years has been the nutrient enrichment of the water. The problem is complex, but high nitrate and phosphate run-offs from the land, coupled with evaporation and low rainfall, lead to algal blooms that de-oxygenate the water, stifling living creatures, particularly fish.

Brixham

Brixham's past has revolved around its fishing activities, which continue to this day. The town claims to be indirectly responsible for establishing Hull and Grimsby as fishing ports on the east coast. From 1780 onwards Brixham boats started fishing off Kent, partly to 'follow the fish' and partly to be near the London market. They then pushed on into the North Sea and claimed to have discovered the fishing grounds there. Their colonising journeys also led to the development of Scarborough and Fleetwood.

Brixham looked very different before about 1800. Like Dartmouth, it has steep hills on all sides, so the inner tidal harbour was filled in for about half a mile (800 metres) – to well past where the Town Hall now stands – to provide flat land. The fine breakwater was started in 1843 and finished in 1916.

The great event in Brixham's history was the landing of the Protestant William of Orange with an army of over 20,000 men on 5 November 1688. He came to oust the Catholic King James from the throne, and the occasion is referred to as the Glorious Revolution. His statue stands on the quay.

Dartmouth

Dartmouth is a deep-water port of great charm and history. In medieval times it was more important in national maritime terms than it is today, although the presence of the Britannia Royal Naval College continues the naval tradition.

The Second and Third Crusades left from Dartmouth – what a chaotic turmoil of people, animals and supplies the port must have witnessed then! Later, trade developed with Spain, Portugal, France and Newfoundland.

When all this was happening, Dartmouth was operating from a very cramped site. To us this gives Dartmouth its potent atmosphere, but merchants and ships' captains needed space, and the steep hills sliding straight into the harbour gave no room to expand. So over hundreds of years Dartmouth has pushed outwards into the estuary. The visitor should realise that all Dartmouth's flat land is in fact made-up land created from the river.

The town is full of fine buildings. The Butterwalk is a Grade I listed building, containing the town museum, and St Saviour's Church has a gallery dating from 1633. Bayard's Cove near the Lower Ferry is powerfully evocative of the rollicking days of sail and some of *The Onedin Line* was filmed there.

The inventor Thomas Newcomen (1663–1729), who produced the first industrial steam engine, was born in Dartmouth. Adjoining the town's Tourist Information Centre is a building housing an early-18th-century example of a Newcomen engine.

The massive Royal Naval College was built only in 1905, although it has been enlarged since. It replaced several superannuated 'wooden walls' – hulks from the days of sail used as accommodation for naval cadets – moored in the Dart.

Pleasure boats leave from the quay in every direction during the summer, and a trip upriver to Totnes is one of Devon's great experiences. Walkers should not try to reach Brixham by boat, as the walk around the cliffs is very special, but to see the shore from the sea having once walked it is a noble ambition.

The boat float at Dartmouth.

10 Brixham to Shaldon

taking in Torquay and its harbour
19³/₄ *miles (31.8 km)*

For most of this next section you are never far away from the seaside resorts of Torbay, but do not let this put you off. In amongst the caravan parks and bed & breakfasts there are fine stretches of sand, elegant Victorian gardens and the start of Devon's famous red sandstone cliffs.

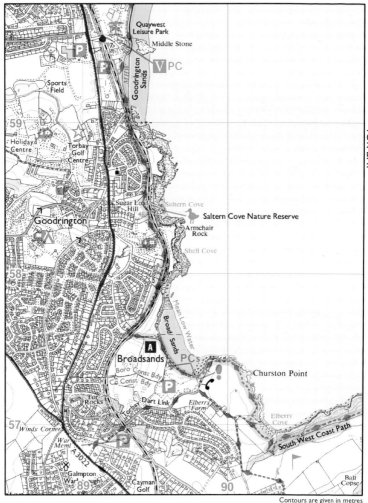

Contours are given in metres
The vertical interval is 10m

From Brixham Quay **67** (*see map below, continuing on page 132*), take the signposted route by the harbour to Oxen Cove and Freshwater Quarry car park. At the far end climb the steps and at a small open area stay up high, and do not be tempted to descend to the first cove, Fishcombe Cove **68**. Carry on above this cove, passing between the chalets to reach a small wood. The path now descends to Churston Cove, which is crossed above the high-water mark.

There now follows a steep but pleasant climb, which leads to a long green corridor between golf course and woodland. At the western end of this stretch the path zigzags down to Elberry Cove. The small ruined building was the bathing and boating station of the Buller family of Lupton House, $1^1/_2$ miles (2.4 km) inland. If the sea is calm you may spot a freshwater spring bubbling to the surface off the beach.

Follow the grassy headland of Churston Point round to the aptly named Broad Sands. (A leaflet describing a circular way-marked walk starting from Broad Sands car park can be purchased from local tourist information centres.) Stay with the sea wall to a point beyond halfway, when you turn away from the beach **A** and head inland along a tarmac track under the railway viaduct. Do not be tempted to ascend the rough land or walk to the far end of the beach.

Having passed beneath the viaduct, turn sharp right up a flight of steps to reach the path beside the railway, then follow it to Goodrington. The railway is, of course, the one you saw earlier at Kingswear. At Goodrington, follow the promenade to the north end, passing in front of the enormous leisure centre and

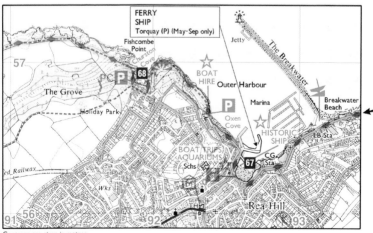

Contours are given in metres
The vertical interval is 10m

Paignton beach and pier.

pub. When faced with Roundham Head, slant up the path through the shrubbery on the steep cliff face, following a trail of acorns set into the pavement.

The path curves round in front of a large house, emerging on Cliff Road. From here it follows the road to Paignton harbour and on to the promenade. The architecture of Paignton is undistinguished, but Kirkham House in Kirkham Street is a 14th-century building, beautifully restored in 1960.

As well as being the terminus of the steam railway that puffs to Kingswear, Paignton is the end of the BR branch line which serves Torquay from Newton Abbot.

Paignton promenade is now followed (using the embedded acorns) to the far end, where a brief diversion inland **B** has to be made round some hotels to reach Preston Sands.

At the far north end of Preston Sands go up steps, then follow a tarmaced path that takes you over Hollicombe Head, turning left over the railway bridge. Now turn right and follow the path through the park, passing the play area to your left. Head for the two big ponds and leave the park via the main gates. Once out on the road turn right.

Having reached the main road, the A379, there is a pavement all the way to Torquay harbour, about 1^1/$_2$ miles (2.4 km). Once past Corbyn's Head the character of Torbay changes, and the elegance one associates with Torquay takes over.

The Coast Path follows the road around Abbey Sands, taking their name from Torre Abbey. The Abbey, originally founded

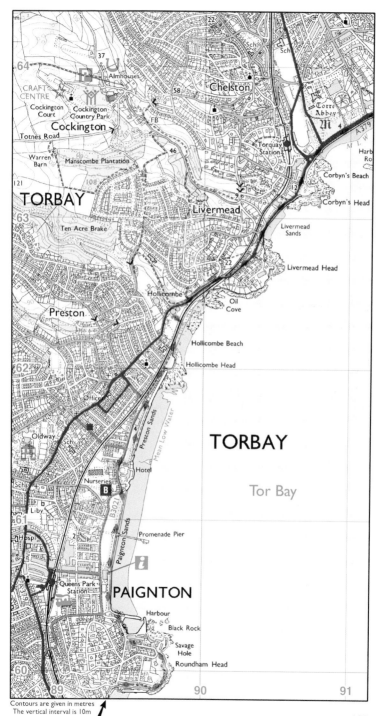

Contours are given in metres
The vertical interval is 10m

135

in 1196, can be found behind the gardens on the left side of the road. The path now goes seaward of the Princess Theatre and through the gardens to the Pavilion, now a shopping mall. This is the centre of Torquay and the path circles the harbour before climbing Beacon Hill up to the Imperial Hotel. Just inside the hotel's main entrance the path goes left, sloping upwards and ending suddenly overlooking London Bridge, a rock arch jutting out into Torbay. Climb the steps 15 yards (14 metres) from the end of the path. These are steep and lead to Rock End gardens through which you thread your way, passing a gazebo, and finally emerging on Daddyhole Plain through an arch at the southern corner.

Leave Daddyhole Plain by steps at the east end and follow a tarmac path down. Enter the path on the right which is signposted to 'Car park Meadfoot Beach' and descend the steps. The impressive Hesketh Crescent, built in 1846, is on the left as you descend. It is now the Osborne Hotel, although part is let as timeshare apartments.

At the east end of the beach go up the path at the back of a small car park; this cuts a corner beneath Kilmorie flats. Follow the road up, facing oncoming traffic.

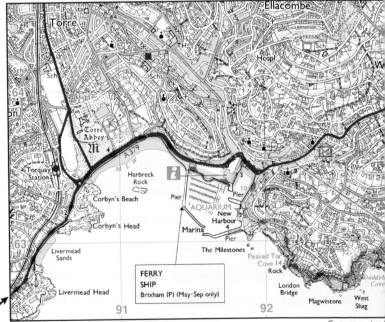

Contours are given i
The vertical interv

You are now on the Marine Drive, opened in 1924. Notice the evergreen holm oaks, which are such a feature here. The path that passes around Thatcher Point is closed off halfway round at the time of writing (2002), so as the road opens out continue along the Marine Drive; 250 yards (230 metres) further on a turning right to Hope's Nose is an optional extra. This path is opposite Thatcher Avenue. Hope's Nose is a low-level promontory that previous generations have done their best to make even smaller. In the 19th century it was extensively quarried and ships came right into the point to be loaded with the limestone. Gold was found here in small but very fine quantities in the early 20th century. Now it is a haven for sea anglers and people seeking a haven from the hustle and bustle of Torquay.

Back on the Marine Drive, follow the footpath north beside the higher side of the road. Where this path rejoins the road, the Coast Path is signposted off to the right, between some houses. It now leads into 'Bishop's Walk' and a very pleasant section of woodland known as Black Head **C**.

The Coast Path now reaches the large car park above Anstey's Cove. Redgate Beach, formerly a popular place for

are given in metres
tical interval is 5m

Oddicombe cliff railway, still working over seventy years after it opened to carry holidaymakers down to the beach.

holidaymakers, is now closed (2002) due to the risk from unstable cliffs behind. The jagged outline of Long Quarry Point is worth noting from Anstey's Cove.

Carrying on from the top of the Anstey's Cove road, turn right (north) and 100 yards (90 metres) further on turn right again up some steps signposted 'Coast Path', and then right at a fork. The path emerges on to Walls Hill, or Babbacombe Downs, and the fence should be followed round to a shelter. Once over the top a good view opens up ahead. All the cliffs you can see ahead of you are red from Oddicombe Beach onwards, except for those at Petit Tor Point, where a massive limestone 'ice-cream scoop' has been quarried out of the cliff. This is known as the Giant's Armchair.

The clifftop hedge should be followed until you see a well-worn path heading into the scrub. Follow this, descending steeply to a minor road. Turn right, then take the path signposted 'Babbacombe Beach'. Turn right again before a stone arch, and take the path which zigzags down many steps to emerge above the beach by the red-tiled Cary Arms **69**. This is the village of Babbacombe. Until Torquay developed as a holiday resort Babbacombe was a small fishing port. The pier was built in 1889.

Walk along behind Babbacombe Beach, then traverse the cliffs via wooden walkways and steps to Oddicombe Beach. Like Redgate Beach, parts of Oddicombe Beach are closed due to rock falls (2002).

To walk the Coast Path onwards from Oddicombe Beach you have to climb up the zigzag road, used for occasional hill-climb competitions, and at the second bend enter a path on the right beside the cliff railway. The cliff railway is similar to the kind

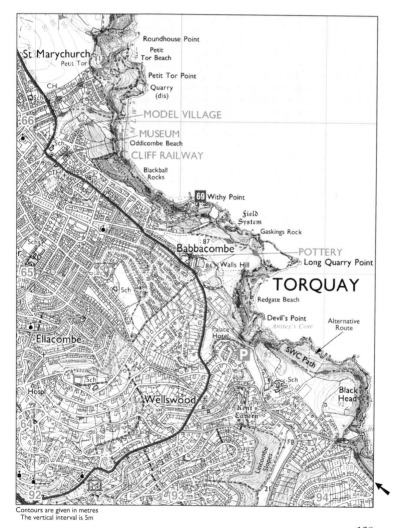

Contours are given in metres
The vertical interval is 5m

found at Lynmouth and Hastings. This one was opened in 1926, carries 40 passengers and averages about 654 miles (1,052 km) each season. You pass beneath the railway, then continue down and up before having to turn inland due to the landslide that has closed Oddicombe Beach. This takes you up the valley and on to the road, where you take the next right and head back down towards Petit Tor.

When the official Coast Path is reached again at the top of a grassy area, carry on north to the right of a typical Torquay Italianate house. Petit Tor can be climbed, but the Coast Path passes to the left of it. Petit Tor marble enjoyed a vogue in the 18th and 19th centuries, but has since passed out of fashion.

The golf course is over the fence on the left, and the way is clear along a wide path showing evidence of badgers, rabbits and moles. At a three-path junction take the right-hand one, and a short distance further on fork right again. Now stay on the main path which contours north. (A lower loop path leaves this one to rejoin it further on.) At a small valley, faced with a choice, go right, and carry on round a long left-hand bend down to the valley road at Watcombe **70**. You may want to consider a detour to Watcombe Park, the estate landscaped by Isambard Kingdom Brunel, who planned his country home there.

Having reached the valley road leading to Watcombe Beach **70**, turn left for 20 yards (18 metres), then right, and climb to the Valley of Rocks. In the bowl, turn right and at a fork bear left, and the path now goes for 50 yards (45 metres) along a ledge hacked out of the cliff. Railings on the inside give security, but anyone lacking a head for heights may have problems here. This is the Goat Path **71**.

The Coast Path reaches a lane, which it now follows briefly. Nowhere else between Torquay and Shaldon is the walker so far from the sea – all of 300 yards (275 metres)! However, at the top of a rise take a stile on the right, which brings you down a lane, then to a fenced-off path that leads along several field edges to Maidencombe. This is the last opportunity for refreshment before the tiring 3$\frac{1}{2}$-mile (5.6-km) switchback cliff-edge path to Shaldon.

Leave Maidencombe by the road going north from the car park entrance, bearing left behind the last house. The route is straightforward now, and just when one is getting jaded with the ups and downs, the Coast Path meets the A379, enters the top field above Shaldon and begins to free-wheel down past the pitch-and-putt course, with encouraging views ahead.

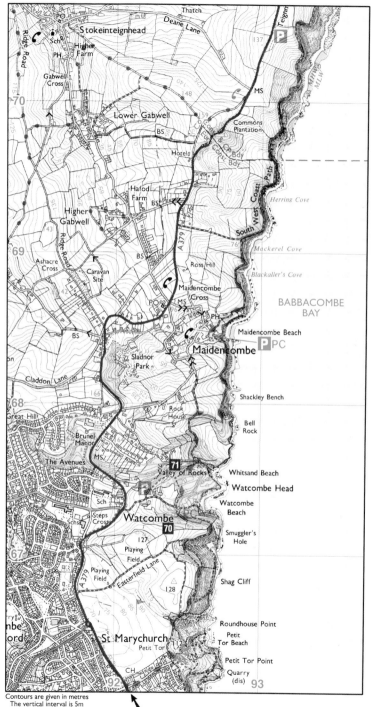

Contours are given in metres
The vertical interval is 5m

Soon after passing into the second pitch-and-putt field, enter a hedge gap on the right, go down some steps and take the gently curving track going down into a deep cutting. When it reaches the pitch-and-putt car park, turn right into the trees. The path leads to the top of the Ness, such a feature in the South Devon landscape. Old prints show the Ness bare of trees; the present grove was planted to mark Queen Victoria's coronation. At the top, turn left and descend to Shaldon, from where the ferry leaves for Teignmouth. (If walking from east to west, leave Shaldon by climbing the Ness, leaving all buildings on your right.)

Between Shaldon and Teignmouth is the shingle bank called the Salty, a firm expanse where fishermen dig for bait between the tides. Beneath the Ness a well-lit pedestrian tunnel probes to a sandy cove known as Ness Beach. This is another designated Eurobeach.

The present bridge dates from 1931, and a toll was collected at the north end until 1948. The walker can reach Teignmouth (see page 154) by the bridge if the ferry is not running (see page 159).

Shaldon Beach with the Ness beyond.

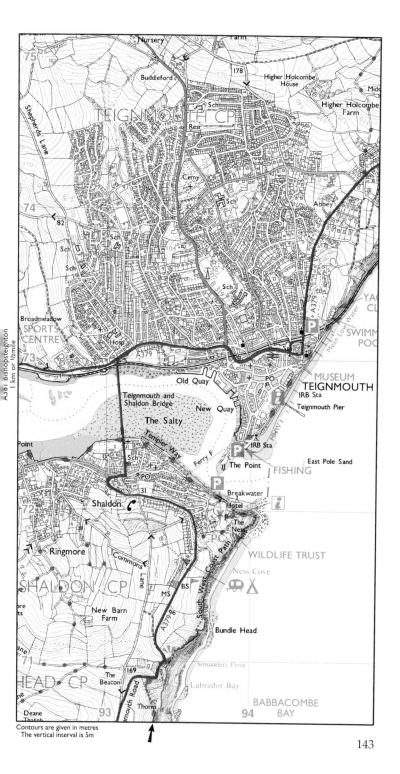

The growth of the South Devon holiday area

The earliest holiday 'resorts' in South Devon were Exmouth and Teignmouth. Dawlish quickly followed, and had a bath house and public rooms by 1812. These three places were handy to Exeter, which at the beginning of the 19th century was a provincial centre of some importance.

The story of Torquay's growth is more complicated, and bedevilled by a kind of mythology which attributed the development of the town to the presence in Torbay of the Channel Fleet during the Napoleonic Wars. The officers are supposed to have lodged their families in the embryo resort.

However, Percy Russell, writing in his scholarly book *A History of Torquay and the Famous Anchorage of Torbay* (1960) found no evidence for this theory, and was firmly of the view that the medical officers on duty with the Fleet understood the climatic benefits of the sheltered site of Torquay and recommended it to their consumptive patients. There can be no doubt that it was as a haven for invalids that Torquay's reputation was made.

Of course, the Napoleonic Wars had closed the Continent to English travellers, and those who had done the Grand Tour saw similarities between the Mediterranean and Torbay. Add to these ingredients the fact that the Palk and Cary families owned much land round Torquay and were ready to sell (at the right price), and we have the makings of Torquay as a fashionable watering place. The final fillip was the kudos provided by a visit from royalty, and in 1833 the future Queen Victoria came to Torquay with her mother.

Ruskin christened Torquay the 'Italy of England' and Italianate residences, with names such as Villa Borghese and Villa Como, sprang up. Napoleon Bonaparte had been brought to Torbay en route to St Helena in 1815 and even he said the scenery reminded him of Porto Ferraio in Elba.

The railway arrived at Torre, Torquay, in 1848, and from then on the population increased rapidly. It took eleven years to push the line on to Paignton, which then became the popular resort on the bay. It had better beaches and a flatter topography. Brixham was a late starter in the holiday stakes, and until the late 1940s was the olde-worlde fishing village that people visited while staying in Torquay or Paignton. But as land was used up elsewhere, post-war development of the chalet kind squeezed into the higher parts of Brixham, and that is what the west-to-east walker sees first.

Dawlish Warren from Langstone Rock, with the Exe Estuary beyond.

Torquay

The rise of Torquay to become Devon's largest holiday resort has just been told briefly. If this gives the impression that the town is a latter-day upstart, it should be pointed out that evidence of human occupation dating back to between 20,000 and 30,000 BC was found when Kent's Cavern was excavated. This cave is situated in that part of Torquay between Meadfoot Beach and Anstey's Cove, and is open to the public.

From about 1200 until the Dissolution of the Monasteries Torre Abbey flourished behind what we now know as Torre Abbey Sands. The tithe barn survives and some of the original buildings have been incorporated into what is now, after many vicissitudes, the borough's art gallery and museum. The little room devoted to Agatha Christie – who was born in Torquay, and lived for many years on the River Dart – is alone worth deviating from the Coast Path to see.

The Coast Path walker is likely to pass the Pavilion, where the Princess Gardens meet the harbour. This singular structure, so elegant and redolent of Torquay's artistic past, is now enjoying a revival as a shopping mall. It was built in 1911 as a concert hall, and famous conductors performed here – Beecham, Boult, Wood and Barbirolli; Elgar also made a guest appearance.

11 Teignmouth to the Exe

via Dawlish and Starcross
7¹/₂ miles (12.1 km)

As long as you time it right, the path from here to the Exe estuary is along the flat, apart from one short climb. It all depends on the tides: the sea wall from Teignmouth to Dawlish and then the section from Dawlish to Dawlish Warren should not be attempted at high tide or in rough weather.

Teignmouth promenade leads to the limestone sea wall which protects the railway from the waves. The railway is the main line between Paddington and Penzance, one of Isambard Kingdom Brunel's great civil-engineering achievements.

The distance from the ferry to the end of the sea wall is very nearly 2 miles (3.2 km), and as you leave the sound of the sea to climb up Smugglers Lane **A** you see one of the five tunnels Brunel had to build to bring the railway round the coast.

Should the tide be high or getting high, then this route, where the path has to go below the railway, is impassable, and

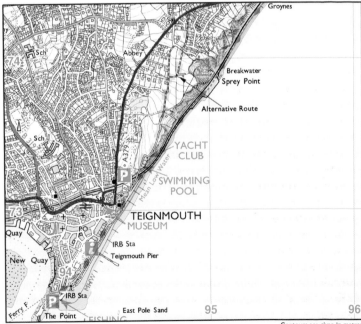

Contours are given in metres
The vertical interval is 5m

146

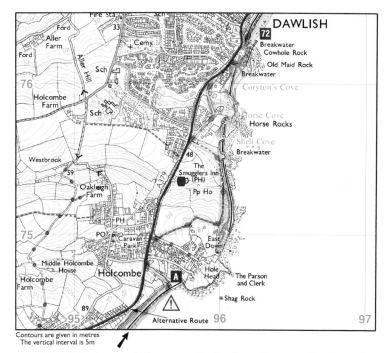

Contours are given in metres
The vertical interval is 5m

considerable time will be spent in backtracking and taking the inland route. This rejoins the Coast Path via the A379.

The route now is up Smugglers Lane **A** to the A379, which is reached opposite a phone box. Turn right (north) and walk up this busy road for 150 yards (135 metres). It may be best to cross to the pavement on the far side, but you will have to re-cross to turn into Derncleugh Gardens. Immediately, go up Windward Lane, and turn left after a few yards. This is a fairly recently opened length of path that is fenced in from the fields, but much better than following the road. The path drops steeply almost to the railway, and climbs up the other side of the valley until a waymark and fingerpost direct the walker inland along a contouring path to a flight of steps and a stile by some old farm buildings. You are thus brought out on to the main road once again, this time opposite South Down Road.

Ignore the new road and stay on Old Teignmouth Road past a toll house, but then the old road peters out and you emerge on the new road once again opposite a bus stop. Stay on the east side of the road, and 20 yards (18 metres) over the top of the hill turn right into a small sitting-out area and a little park. Follow the cliff edge down past two lookouts converted into seat shelters, then down a zigzag path to Dawlish boat cove **72**.

Dawlish remains a pleasant family holiday resort, and is famous for the black swans that paddle around in the Dawlish Water (the Brook).

Heading east from Dawlish you are once again on the sea wall, and a similar warning to that given at Teignmouth applies here: there is a 300-yard (275-metre) stretch of sea wall, just east of Dawlish Station, which is impassable at high tide. Notices at Dawlish Station underpass and at Langstone Rock (to the east) warn of the danger of attempting this stretch at high tide.

If the tide is low there are no problems and Dawlish Warren Station, 1³/₄ miles (2.8 km) from Dawlish Station, can be reached very easily. If the tide is high you will have to follow the Exeter road out of Dawlish and, where it bears inland **B**, a footpath sign near the Rockstone Hotel shows the way to go. This path runs parallel to the railway and just above it. The sea wall and the inland path meet just south of Dawlish Warren Station – those walking the sea wall path should cross to the west side of the railway by the footbridge – and go past a caravan site to the roundabout in the middle of the Dawlish Warren built-up area.

The sandstone cliffs to the west of Dawlish.

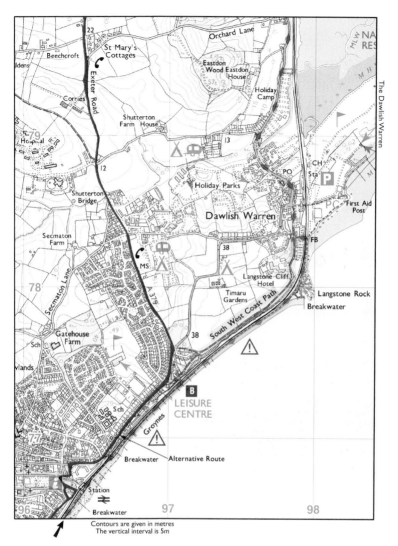

Contours are given in metres
The vertical interval is 5m

Dawlish Warren is a popular resort specialising in chalet, caravan and camping holidays for families. The extensive beach is a designated Eurobeach. A walk out to the end of the Warren itself, the sand bar across the mouth of the Exe, takes one away from humanity to possibly the best bird-watching site along this stretch of the Coast Path. The area is a nature reserve, and part is a golf course. At the far end of the golf course is a two-storey bird hide, which is open to the public. Vast numbers of birds can be seen, and flocks of 20,000 at a time are not unusual. Orchids are abundant, and the tree lupin is a local curiosity.

Powderham Church.

To reach Starcross there is no alternative except to walk along what can be a busy road past Cockwood, where some pleasant pubs provide opportunities for refreshment. At Starcross the ferry crosses the River Exe to Exmouth (see pages 159-60), from where the Coast Path continues on its way to Poole. For the final section of the South West Coast Path, you will need volume number 11 in the National Trail Guide series.

If you intend to cross the Exe at Topsham, carry on up the estuary. The Coast Path officially ends at Starcross.

Beyond stretches the Exe Valley Way, a 9-mile (14.4-km) flat walk along the estuary and canal to Exeter. From Starcross car park, north of the station, head north following the waymarks. This is a fairly busy road, and there are no views over the estuary

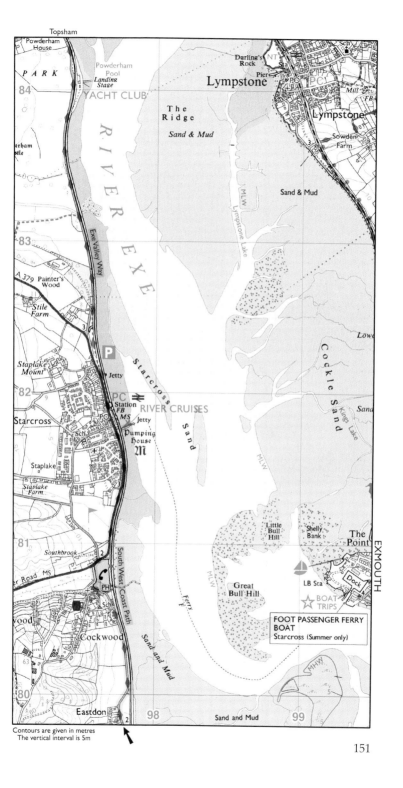

Contours are given in metres
The vertical interval is 5m

The atmospheric railway pumping house at Starcross.

for the pedestrian, but for 1 mile (1.6 km) Powderham Park is on the west of the road. Look out here for the herd of fallow deer and glimpses of Powderham Castle through the ancient oaks. Powderham Castle has been the home of the Courtenay family, the Earls of Devon, since 1390, and successive generations have each made their own contribution to a building which is now a hotch-potch of various architectural styles. There is a heronry at Powderham.

When the road reaches Powderham Church, the Exe Valley Way carries on alongside the railway line. A short digression to view the church and the fine avenue of evergreen oaks is well worth making and will not add a great deal of time.

The path crosses the railway by a level crossing where great care is needed, as the high-speed trains seem to approach quite silently, and carries on north along Powderham Bank. A plaque states that the present sea wall was built in 1963. The outlet of Exeter Canal is reached at Turf Lock, where there is a pub. From this point the canal, with the oldest pound lock in England, built in 1564–6, stretches $5^{1}/_{2}$ miles (8.8 km) to Exeter.

From Turf, where there are usually boats moored, the best way forward is up the west towpath to the bridge over the canal at Topsham Lock. There is a public right of way along the east bank, but from spring to about August the vegetation is allowed to grow. This encourages people to walk up the other towpath, so avoiding disturbance to the breeding birds along this side of the estuary. About $1^{1}/_{2}$ miles (2.4 km) north of Turf you reach the bridge giving access to the east side of the canal. From here a small ferry crosses the River Exe to Topsham at the times advertised (see page 160).

Exeter Youth Hostel is at Countess Wear, on the outskirts of the city, about 2 miles (3.2 km) north-west of Topsham Lock.

You do not have to cross the river here. The towpath can be traced right up to Exeter, passing under the M5 motorway and by the Double Locks wetlands and pub of the same name. At Exeter the rejuvenated quayside area offers bars, restaurants and craft shops, whilst the city centre is worth a visit, if only to view the cathedral.

Brunel's 'atmospheric railway'

Brunel decided to power his trains along this part of the railway on 'atmospheric' principles. A continuous pipe with a longitudinal slot along the top was laid between the rails, and in this pipe ran a piston fitted to the leading vehicle in the train. Stationary steam engines in pumping houses – and Starcross is the last surviving one to have actually worked – pumped out the air in front of the piston, thus forming a vacuum, while air coming in naturally behind the piston pushed the train forward.

In theory the idea was brilliant. It was clean, and when it worked the trains ran speedily and quietly, but Brunel did not have the materials to match the concept. The longitudinal slit along the top of the pipe was sealed with a leather flap valve, and the salt atmosphere and a chemical reaction rapidly rotted the leather. A lubricant was therefore applied to the flap, but this succeeded only in attracting rats and mice, which got sucked into the tube, jamming the pistons, and then got blown out into the pumping houses!

The system operated only between Exeter and Teignmouth, and nine trains a day achieved speeds of 70 mph, but so great were the problems that Brunel recommended it be scrapped. A loss of £426,368 was incurred on what became known as the 'atmospheric caper', and conventional locomotives took over.

For some years in the 1980s, the Starcross pumping house was a well-organised museum of the atmospheric railway, but it has since closed.

Teignmouth

Teignmouth is Devon's second oldest holiday resort (after Exmouth), but it had a considerable history before it added summer visitors to its other businesses. A fishing industry was there from early times, and trade with Newfoundland developed in the 18th century. It also exported ball clay, granite and timber, and ships were built on the banks of the Teign. The continuity of its trade is remarkable, for while only a small amount of fishing is now done, Teignmouth is the main exporting port for the ball clay that is mined near Newton Abbot and north of Okehampton. So, on to the coarse industrial base was grafted the elegance that late-18th-century visitors expected. Modern recreational activities such as sailing, wind-surfing and sea angling have now broken the barriers somewhat and take place cheek-by-jowl with the ball-clay ships.

PART THREE

USEFUL
INFORMATION

Transport

Rail

Rail services to this stretch of the Coast Path are fairly limited. Falmouth, across the Fal from the starting point, can be reached by a branch line from the main line at Truro. The mainline station at Par is just a five-minute walk from the Coast Path. Until Plymouth is reached, the only other place on the Coast Path to have a direct rail link is Looe. The branch line for Looe starts on the main line at Liskeard. Plymouth, of course, has frequent trains, but the next places to have full British Rail services are Paignton and Torquay. Teignmouth, Dawlish, Dawlish Warren and Starcross are on the main line, but express trains do not stop at these stations, and the last two have a very sketchy service, although it is better in the summer. Exmouth and Topsham are reached by train from Exeter. For timetable and fare enquiries phone 08457 484950 (24-hour service).

The privately owned Torbay and Dartmouth Steam Railway runs between Paignton and Kingswear (for Dartmouth) at Easter, and then from May to early October.

Buses

The larger centres in Cornwall and Devon, not necessarily on the Coast Path, are served by express coach services from all parts of the country. However, once at places such as Truro, Bodmin, Liskeard, Plymouth and Totnes, it is less easy to find convenient bus links to the coast.

The coastline from Torcross, through Dartmouth to Brixham, Torquay, Teignmouth and Starcross is, however, never far from a main road along which buses run at all seasons.

The Cornwall Passenger Transport Unit at County Hall, Truro, publishes comprehensive public-transport timetables every year. There are five separate volumes covering different areas of Cornwall; each costs £1.50 and includes a county map. These are available from local tourist information centres and bus stations. The office will answer enquiries over the telephone. For further details contact the Passenger Transport Unit, Cornwall County Council, County Hall, Truro, TR1 3AY. Tel. (01872) 322000.

In Devon there is no comprehensive timetable published *at the time of writing*. However, the Transport Co-ordination Centre at County Hall, Exeter, produces a series of area timetables which they can send to enquirers who write or phone, and of course visitors can enquire locally at tourist information centres or bus stations.

The same office publishes a 197-page volume useful for disabled people called *A Guide to Transport Services in Devon: With particular reference to rural communities, elderly and disabled people* (Devon County Council, 1993). For further details of public transport contact the Transport Co-ordination Centre, Devon County Council, County Engineering & Planning Department, Lucombe House, County Hall, Exeter, EX2 4QW, or Travel Line, tel. 0870 608 2608.

Ferries and river crossings

For complex geomorphological reasons the south-west peninsula slopes from north to south. This means that the rivers flowing south are generally longer than those flowing towards the Bristol Channel. Rising sea level following the end of the last glaciation – and still continuing – has flooded valleys, forming rias or drowned river valleys. The combination of longer rivers and rising sea level is the cause of this estuary proliferation.

From Falmouth to Topsham or Exmouth there are 13 water obstacles, and only at Looe and Shaldon are there bridges. The long-distance walker must therefore take account of these diffi-culties and plan the journey accordingly. The addresses and times given overleaf were updated in 2002. They may well change from year to year. In all cases the qualification 'weather permitting' applies. The crossings are described from west to east, and an indication of the other seasonal boat trips available along the coast is also given. The use of any of these would materially shorten the walk. For up-to-date information, refer to the nearest tourist information centre (TIC).

RIVER FAL (CARRICK ROADS) *Falmouth to St Mawes*

Contact: St Mawes Ferry Co., Prince of Wales Pier, Falmouth. Tel. (01326) 313234.

This is a year-round service operating seven days a week. Leaflets giving times are available locally, but walkers are warned that during the summer ferries do leave Falmouth at two different departure points at opposite ends of the town – Custom House Quay and Prince of Wales Pier.

PERCUIL RIVER *St Mawes to Place*

Contact: Balcomb Boats, tel. (01209) 214901.

Summer-only service, early May to end of September. Check the service before arriving at Place, as there is no phone there. The widely distributed timetable also gives details of walks in the Roseland area. For the water taxi service (when ferry is not running) call: 07970 242258.

RIVER FOWEY *Fowey to Polruan*

Contact: Polruan Ferry Co. Ltd, Tomsyard, East Street, Polruan, PL23 1PB. Tel. (01726) 870232.

Operates all year round, apart from Christmas Day. The ferry departs Fowey from Whitehouse Quay in the summer, and from Town Quay during the winter. Signs are exhibited.

LOOE RIVER *West Looe to East Looe*

The river can be crossed on foot by the bridge which takes the A387 across the harbour, but in the peak summer season a small ferry shuttles across the mouth of the harbour.

RIVER TAMAR *Cremyll to Stonehouse*

Contact: Cremyll Ferry, Cremyll, Torpoint, Cornwall. Tel. (01752) 822105.

Operates all year round, seven days a week, at regular intervals.

In the summer a boat ferries people between Sutton Harbour (Plymouth) and Cawsand.

RIVER PLYM *Plymouth (Sutton Harbour) to Mountbatten*

Contact: 07930 838614.

This service runs from Sutton Harbour taxi pontoon, near the Mayflower Steps, to Mountbatten pontoon.

RIVER YEALM *Warren Point to Noss Mayo slip*

Contact: Mr Gregor, Leaside, Yealm Road, Newton Ferrers, PL8 1DW. Tel. (01752) 872318 / 880079.

Seasonal. Early April to the end of September. For those approaching from the west, ferry times are displayed in the Wembury Beach car park. Shout 'Ferry' at Warren Point.

RIVER ERME *Mothecombe to Wonwell*

There is no ferry, and the only way to cross is to wade the river one hour each side of low water from slipway to slipway. Take great care when floodwater is coming down the Erme or if waves are coming in from the sea. There is no other way to get to the other side short of walking through the lanes to Sequer's Bridge on the A379. Times of low water are shown on ferry information boards on the Avon and Yealm Estuaries. Alternatively, consult a local TIC in advance.

RIVER AVON *Cockleridge to Bantham*

Contact: N. Schroeter, Marsh Cottage, Fore Street, Avetongifford, TQ7 4LR. Tel. (01548) 561196.

Seasonal. Not Sundays. Easter, then May to early September.

Wading the Avon at low tide is not recommended. Do not attempt it. The Avon Estuary Walk provides a 9-mile (14.5 km) alternative way to Bantham via Aveton Gifford. The route is waymarked and details are shown on information boards at each end.

SALCOMBE HARBOUR *Salcombe to East Portlemouth*

Contact: Salcombe Ferry, North Lodge, Landmark Road, Salcombe, TQ8 8NY. Tel. (01548) 842061/842364.

Operates all the year round. In the summer a boat ferries people between Salcombe and South Sands Beach. Contact: Mr Tucker, tel. (01548) 561035.

RIVER DART *Dartmouth to Kingswear*

Contact: South Hams District Council, Lower Ferry Office, The Square, Kingswear, TQ6 0AA. Tel. (01803) 752342.

The Lower Ferry runs all year round. A passenger ferry also crosses to Kingswear from Dartmouth boat float, and the Higher Ferry (vehicle) crosses further up the river. In summer a boat ferries people between Dartmouth and Dartmouth Castle, and boats also run between Dartmouth and Torbay, and between Dartmouth and Totnes.

TOR BAY *Brixham to Torquay*

In the summer a regular service of comfortable vessels takes passengers across Tor Bay. Details of all these services can be obtained from local tourist information centres.

RIVER TEIGN *Shaldon to Teignmouth*

Contact: James Trout, tel. 07880 713420.

All the year round. Saturdays or Sundays during the winter subject to weather.

RIVER EXE *Dawlish Warren to Exmouth*

Contact: Exe Water Taxis, 60 High Street, Topsham, Exeter, EX3 0DY. Tel. 07970 918418.

The water taxi may be able to collect a walker from the east end of Dawlish Warren if arranged in advance. April to mid-October.

RIVER EXE *Starcross to Exmouth*

Contact: Mr B. Rackley, Starcross Pier & Ferry Co., 26 Marine Parade, Dawlish, EX7 9DL. Tel. (01392) 277888.
Seasonal. Early May to mid-October.

RIVER EXE *Topsham Lock to Topsham*

Contact: Exeter City Council Canals and Rivers Department. Tel. (01392) 274306.
Operates Easter to end September every day except Tuesdays, and at weekends in winter dependent on tide and weather.

Accommodation contacts

A list of tourist information centres (TICs) is given below; they will answer enquiries about accommodation, including camping. It is best to approach the TIC nearest to the place you wish to stay. Note that not all TICs are open throughout the year. Most operate (for a fee) a 'book a bed ahead' service for personal callers for the same or the next night. Finding accommodation in the peak holiday period is not easy, so booking in advance is recommended.

Youth hostels and camp sites are noted on the Ordnance Survey maps in this guide, although the walker will find that many additional camp sites spring up during the summer. The solitary backpacker may be able to camp in a farmer's field, but permission should always be obtained first.

The Ramblers' Association yearbook and South West Coast Path Association guidebook – both published annually – list bed and breakfast places (see useful addresses on page 165).

Tourist information centres (TICs) – from west to east
* = open in the summer months only

Cornwall

Falmouth TIC, 28 Killigrew Street, Falmouth, TR11 3PN.
Tel. (01326) 312300.

Fowey TIC, The Post Office, 4 Custom House Hill, Fowey, PL23 1AB. Tel. (01726) 833616.

Looe TIC, The Guildhall, Fore Street, East Looe, PL13 1AA.
Tel. (01503) 262072.

Truro TIC, Municipal Buildings, Boscawen Street, Truro, TR1 2NE. Tel. (01872) 274555.

Mevagissey TIC, West Quay, Mevagissey, PL26 6UJ.
Tel. (01726) 844857.

St Austell TIC, By-Pass, Southborne Road, St Austell, PL25 4RS. Tel. (01726) 879500.

Devon

Plymouth TIC, Island House, 9 The Barbican, Plymouth, PL1 2LS. Tel. (01752) 266030.

Plymouth Discovery Centre, Crabtree, Plymouth, PL3 6RN. Tel. (01752) 266030.

Salcombe TIC, Council Hall, Market Street, Salcombe, TQ8 8DE. Tel. (01548) 843927.

Dartmouth TIC, The Engine House, Mayor's Avenue, Dartmouth, TQ6 9YY. Tel. (01803) 834224.

Brixham TIC, The Old Market House, The Quay, Brixham, TQ5 8TB. Tel. (01803) 852861.

Paignton TIC, The Esplanade, Paignton, TQ4 6ED. Tel. (01803) 558383.

Torquay TIC, Vaughan Parade, Torquay, TQ2 5JG. Tel. (01803) 297428.

Teignmouth TIC, The Den, Sea Front, Teignmouth, TQ14 8BE. Tel. (01626) 215666.

Dawlish TIC, The Lawn, Dawlish, EX7 9EL. Tel. (01626) 215665.

Exmouth TIC, Alexandra Terrace, Exmouth, EX8 1NZ. Tel. (01395) 222299.

The tourist boards associated with these information centres are:

Cornwall Tourist Board, Pydar House, Pydar Street, Truro, TR1 1EA. Tel. (01872) 322900.

South West Tourism, Woodwater Park, Exeter, EX2 5WT. Tel. 0870 4420830.

Looking west from Tregantle Cliffs, with the rifle range on the right.

Facilities for walkers

Once a place reaches a certain size a walker may expect it to have the facilities of car park, pub and toilets, and towns such as Looe, Dartmouth and Torquay have many of these.

Rather than mask other detail on the maps with a multiplicity of symbols, the towns and villages that fall into this category are listed below. Some are slightly off the path, and others, such as Millendreath and Challaborough, which are totally given over to holiday business, may have facilities that are closed out of season.

Cornwall
St Mawes
Portscatho
Gerrans –
   slightly off the
   Coast Path
Portloe
Gorran Haven
Mevagissey
Pentewan
Charlestown
Par
Polkerris
Fowey
Polruan
Polperro
West Looe
East Looe
Millendreath
Downderry

Portwrinkle
Crafthole –
   slightly off the
   Coast Path
Cawsand
Kingsand
Cremyll

Devon
Plymouth
Turnchapel
Wembury
Noss Mayo –
   slightly off the
   Coast Path
Challaborough
Bigbury-on-Sea
Bantham
Outer Hope
Salcombe

East Prawle –
   slightly off the
   Coast Path
Beesands
Torcross
Strete
Stoke Fleming
Dartmouth
Kingswear
Brixham
Paignton
Torquay
Babbacombe
Maidencombe
Shaldon
Teignmouth
Dawlish
Dawlish Warren
Starcross

Useful addresses

The Association of Lightweight Campers, c/o The Camping & Caravanning Club, Greenfields House, Westwood Way, Coventry, CV4 8JH. Tel. (024) 7669 4995.

Caradon Coast and Countryside Service, S.E. Cornwall Discovery Centre, Millpool, West Looe, PL13 2AF. Tel. (01503) 263266.

Cornwall County Council, County Hall, Truro, TR1 3AY. Tel. (01872) 322000.

Cornwall Wildlife Trust, Five Acres, Allet, Truro, TR4 9DJ.
Tel. (01872) 273939.

Countryside Agency (headquarters), John Dower House,
Crescent Place, Cheltenham, Glos, GL50 3RA.
Tel. (01242) 521381.

Countryside Agency, South West Regional Office, 11–15 Dix's
Field, Exeter, EX1 1QA. Tel. (01392) 477150.

Devon Wildlife Trust, 35–37 St David's Hill, Exeter, EX4 4DA.
Tel. (01392) 279244.

Mount Edgcumbe Country Park, Cremyll, Torpoint, Cornwall,
PL10 1HZ. Tel. (01752) 822236. Publishes theme leaflets on a
variety of topics.

National Trust, Cornwall Office, Lanhydrock, Bodmin,
PL30 4DE. Tel. (01208) 74281. Publishes leaflets about its
properties along the coast.

National Trust, Devon Office, Killerton House, Broadclyst,
Exeter, EX5 3LE. Tel. (01392) 881691. Publishes leaflets about
its properties along the coast.

English Nature, Level 2, Renslade House, Bonhay Road, Exeter,
EX4 3AW. Tel. (01392) 889770.

Ordnance Survey, Romsey Road, Maybush, Southampton,
SO16 4GU. Tel. 08456 050505.

Ramblers' Association, Camelford House, 2nd Floor, 87–90
Albert Embankment, London, SE1 7TW. Tel. (020) 7339 8500.
Their annual yearbook has many bed and breakfast addresses.
Available free to members; available to non-members from
major bookshops and newsagents for £4.99 (2002 price).

Royal Society for the Protection of Birds, South West Regional
Office, Keble House, Southernhay Gardens, Exeter, EX1 1NT.
Tel. (01392) 432691.

South West Coast Path Team, c/o Devon County Council,
County Hall, Exeter, EX2 4QW. Tel. (01392) 383560.
E-mail: swcpteam@devon.gov.uk. Co-ordinates the
management of the National Trail.

South Devon Coast & Countryside Service, Follaton House,
Plymouth Road, Totnes, TQ9 5NE. Tel. (01803) 861234.
Publishes a set of nine leaflets about the Coast Path from
Brixham to Plymouth.

South West Coast Path Association, Liz Wallis, Administrator,
Windlestraw, Penquit, Devon, PL21 0LU. Tel./Fax. (01752)
896237. E-mail: info@swcp.org.uk. The Association exists to
help those who enjoy walking this path.

Torbay Coast and Countryside Trust, Cockington Court, Cockington, Torquay, TQ2 6XA. Tel. (01803) 606035.
Youth Hostels Association, National Office, Trevelyan House, Dimple Road, Matlock, Derbyshire, DE4 3YH. Tel. (01629) 529600.

Guided walks

The management and interpretive provision of this stretch of the Coast Path – except on National Trust land, which is looked after by the Trust – is split between Cornwall County Council, the Caradon Coast and Countryside Service, the South Devon Coast and Countryside Service and the Torbay Coast and Countryside Trust.

These services organise guided walks conducted by local experts on a wide range of topics, not necessarily in the summer only. They could be general interest walks led by National Trust wardens or local ramblers, or specialist walks, talks, and boat trips, on everything from astronomy to exploring rock pools. There may be a small charge. Leaflets listing these outings can be picked up at information centres, libraries, museums and cafés, or from the offices of the various services (see pages 161, 164 and 165).

Bibliography

Barber, Chips, *The Torbay Book* (Obelisk Publications, 1984).
—— and Chard, Judy, *Burgh Island and Bigbury Bay* (Obelisk Publications, 1988).
Carne, Tony, *Cornwall's Forgotten Corner* (Lodenek Press, 1985).
Clarke, Jennifer, *Exploring the West Country: A Woman's Guide* (Virago, 1987).
Davies, Stan, *Wildlife of the Exe Estuary* (Harbour Books, 1987).
Delderfield, Eric R., *Torbay Story* (Raleigh Press, 1951).
Devon County Council, *Coastlines of Devon* (Devon County Council, 1980).
Dickinson, M.G. (ed.), *A Living from the Sea* (Devon Books, 1987).
du Maurier, Daphne, *Rebecca* (Gollancz, 1938).
—— *The House on the Strand* (Gollancz, 1969; Pan, 1979).
English Heritage, *Register of Parks and Gardens of Special Historic Interest*, Cornwall and Devon entries (English Heritage, 1987).

Fedden, Robin and Joekes, Rosemary, *The National Trust Guide* (Jonathan Cape, 1973/84).

Grigson, Geoffrey, *Freedom of the Parish* (Phoenix House, 1954).

Harvey, Phil and Keene, Peter, *Prawle Peninsula Landscape Trail* (Field Studies Council, 1985).

Hoskins, W.G., *Devon* (Collins, 1954).

Hunt, Peter (ed.), *Devon's Age of Elegance* (Devon Books, 1984).

Langley, Martin and Small, Edwina, *Estuary & River Ferries of South West England* (Waine Research Publications, 1984).

—— *Lost Ships of the West Country* (Stanford Maritime, 1988).

Larn, Richard, *The Diver Guide to South Cornwall* (Underwater World Publications, 1983).

—— and Carter, Clive, *Cornish Shipwrecks Vol 1: The South Coast* (David & Charles, 1971).

Le Messurier, Brian, *The Visitor's Guide to Devon* (Landmark Publishing, fourth edition, 1999).

Luck, Liz, *South Cornish Harbours* (A. & C. Black, 1988).

McDonald, Kendall and Cockbill, Derek, *The Diver Guide to South Devon* (Underwater World Publications, 1982).

Padel, O.J., *A Popular Dictionary of Cornish Place-Names* (Alison Hodge, 1988).

Perkins, John W., *Geology Explained in South and East Devon* (David & Charles, 1971).

Pevsner, Nikolaus (revised by Enid Radcliffe), *The Buildings of England: Cornwall* (Penguin Books, 1983).

—— *The Buildings of England: Devon* (Penguin Books, second edition, with Bridget Cherry, 1989).

Pope, Rita Tregellas, *The Visitor's Guide to Cornwall and the Isles of Scilly* (Landmark Publishing, fourth edition, 1999).

Shallcross, Martyn, *Daphne du Maurier Country* (Bossiney Books, 1987).

Soper, Tony, *Wildlife of the Dart Estuary* (Harbour Books, 1982).

—— and Le Messurier, Brian, *The National Trust Guide to the Coast* (Webb & Bower, second impression, 1986).

Travis, J.T., *The Rise of the Devon Seaside Resorts* (University of Exeter, 1993).

Weatherhill, Craig, *Cornovia: Ancient Sites of Cornwall and Scilly* (Alison Hodge, 1985).

Wills, Graham (ed.), *Devon Estuaries* (Devon Books, 1985).

Ordnance Survey Maps covering the South West Coast Path (Falmouth to Exmouth)

Landranger Maps: 192, 200, 201, 202, 204.

Explorer Maps: OL20, South Devon – Brixham to Newton Ferrers, 30 Exmouth & Sidmouth, 31 Torquay & Dawlish, 103 The Lizard, 105 Falmouth & Mevagissey, 107 St Austell & Liskeard, 108 Lower Tamar Valley.

Motoring Maps: Reach the South West Coast Path by car using Routemaster Map 8, 'South West England and South Wales'.